I Talk to Myself Too Much

"Your Inner Dialogue: Exploring the World of Self Talk"

Dr Robert J Glen

I Talk to Myself Too Much

Copyright © 2024 by Dr Robert J Glen

Dedication

To all the solitary dreamers and midnight problem-solvers, who find solace in their own voices and company in their inner dialogues.

To those who, like RJ, navigate the delicate balance between eccentricity and introspection, and discover that sometimes, the most profound conversations are the ones we have with ourselves.

May you always find humor and clarity in your journey, and may your inner monologues lead you to unexpected revelations and victories.

Table of Contents

Part I: The Awakening

RJ's Journey into Self-Talk

RJ's Journey into self-talk is filled with moments of amusing monologues and unexpected companionship. Picture this: a middle-aged software engineer living alone, coding late into the night, muttering bug fixes to himself while celebrating tiny victories when his program compiles. It's a scene that seems almost cinematic, yet it's RJ's daily reality. His life in a quiet apartment sets the stage for a behavior that emerges slowly at first. What begins as sporadic murmurings during work gradually infiltrates other aspects of his routine, like cooking dinner and running errands. Whether he's debugging code or deciding what to have for lunch, his habit of talking to himself becomes a source of constant chatter and entertainment.

In Part I, we delve into RJ's growing self-talk behavior and explore its implications on his solo lifestyle. We'll follow him as he navigates through humorous moments and subtle transformations, starting with brief, often unnoticed self-dialogues that evolve into extended conversations. Some in front of a mirror. By examining how his verbal exchanges extend beyond work hours and into everyday activities, you'll gain insights into how self-talk serves as both a coping mechanism and a creative outlet for RJ. Additionally, we'll touch on the challenges and gradual realizations he faces as this behavior becomes an integral part of his daily routine. Get ready to dive into a story that blends humor with introspection, offering a unique perspective on the power of our inner voice.

The 'Self-Talk' Evolution

RJ's journey into the world of self-talk began on an ordinary Tuesday evening. Picture this: a middle-aged software engineer, living alone in a modest apartment, surrounded by the soft glow of computer screens and the gentle whirring of cooling fans. Little did RJ know that this unremarkable evening would mark the beginning of an extraordinary adventure into the realm of internal dialogue.

It all started with a particularly stubborn bug in his code. RJ had been staring at the same lines for hours, his eyes growing ever more bloodshot as the night wore on. Frustrated and caffeinated, he suddenly burst out:

"Oh, come on! What are you, some kind of digital Houdini? Show yourself, you sneaky little semicolon!"

Startled by the sound of his own voice in the quiet room, RJ glanced around, half-expecting to see a coworker he'd forgotten about. But no, he was alone – just him and the mischievous code that seemed to be taunting him from the screen.

With a shrug, RJ decided to roll with it. "Alright, Mr. Code," he continued, leaning back in his chair, "let's talk this out. What exactly are you trying to accomplish by not working, hm? Are you staging a digital rebellion? Advocating for better working conditions for algorithms everywhere?"

As ridiculous as it felt, RJ found that talking through the problem out loud was oddly helpful. He began to see connections he'd missed before, and within minutes, he'd tracked down the elusive bug.

"Aha!" he exclaimed triumphantly, pointing at the screen. "Thought you could hide from me, did you? Well, nobody expects the Spanish Inquisition – or the RJ Inquisition, for that matter!"

As he basked in the glow of victory (and multiple computer screens), RJ realized that this one-sided conversation had not only solved his problem but had also been strangely entertaining. Little did he know, this was just the beginning of his chatty new relationship with himself.

Over the next few weeks, RJ's self-talk began to spill over into other areas of his life. His morning routine became a one-man show, complete with commentary and sound effects:

"And now, ladies and gentlemen," RJ announced to his empty bathroom, his toothbrush doubling as a microphone, "watch in amazement as the incredible RJ attempts to style his hair without looking like he stuck his finger in an electrical socket!"

He paused dramatically, holding up a comb like a magician about to perform a grand illusion.

"Will he succeed? Or will he be forced to wear a hat for the third day in a row? The tension is unbearable!"

Even grocery shopping became an adventure in self-narration. RJ found himself providing color commentary on his own indecisiveness:

"RJ approaches the cereal aisle with caution," he muttered under his breath, pushing his cart slowly. "The choices are overwhelming. Will he go for the sensible bran flakes, or will he throw caution to the wind and opt for the sugar-laden, artificially colored puffs of childhood nostalgia?"

He stood there, hands on hips, engaged in an intense internal debate about the merits of fiber versus fun. Other shoppers gave him a wide berth, clearly concerned about the man having an existential crisis in front of the Froot Loops.

"The crowd is on the edge of their seats," RJ continued, oblivious to the stares. "In a shocking twist, he reaches for both! It's madness, ladies and gentlemen! The cereal world will never be the same!"

As he triumphantly tossed both boxes into his cart, RJ caught the eye of a bewildered stock boy. "Just keeping myself entertained," he explained with a sheepish grin, quickly pushing his cart towards the relative safety of the produce section.

But it wasn't all fun and games. RJ soon discovered that his newfound habit had its challenges, particularly in public spaces. Like the time he was deeply engrossed in a self-debate about the merits of various programming languages while riding the bus:

"Sure, Python, you're user-friendly and versatile," he mused out loud, "but can you match the speed and efficiency of C++? I think not!"

It was only when he noticed the entire bus had fallen silent, all eyes on him, that RJ realized he'd been gesticulating wildly and speaking at full volume. The elderly lady next to him clutched her purse a little tighter, eyeing him warily.

"Um, just practicing for a... debate," RJ offered weakly. "About... snakes. And plus signs."

The lady didn't look convinced, but RJ was saved from further explanation as his stop approached. He hurried off the bus, his face burning with embarrassment, vowing to keep his programming language dissertations to himself in the future – or at least invest in some less conspicuous earbuds to make it look like he was on a phone call.

Despite these occasional social hiccups, RJ found that his self-talk habit was becoming an integral part of his daily life. It helped him solve problems, made mundane tasks more entertaining, and provided companionship in his solitary lifestyle. Sure, he might look a little eccentric talking to himself in the checkout line or having animated debates with his houseplants, but RJ was starting to think that a little eccentricity was a small price to pay for the benefits of his inner dialogue.

As he settled into bed one night, exhausted but amused by his day of internal conversations, RJ couldn't help but chuckle at the bizarre turn his life had taken.

"Well, RJ," he said to himself, staring at the ceiling with a grin, "looks like you've officially gone off the deep end. But hey, at least you'll always have someone interesting to talk to!"

With that, he rolled over and drifted off to sleep, his mind already buzzing with the conversations tomorrow would bring. RJ's journey into self-talk was well and truly underway, and life would never be the same again.

The Emerging Pattern: RJ's Self-Talk

As days turned into weeks, RJ's self-talk habit began to evolve in ways he never expected. What started as simple muttering during coding sessions had blossomed into a full-fledged internal dialogue that touched every aspect of his life. It was as if he'd unlocked a hidden level in the video game of life, and the new challenge was navigating the world with a constantly chattering sidekick – himself.

One sunny Saturday morning, RJ decided it was time to tackle the long-avoided task of cleaning his apartment. As he surveyed the chaos of his living room, he couldn't help but channel his inner nature documentary narrator:

"And here we see the elusive 'Programmer in his Natural Habitat,'" RJ intoned in his best David Attenborough impression. "Note the precarious stacks of pizza boxes, forming a sort of modern art installation we'll call 'Leaning Tower of Grease-a.' To the left, we observe the rare 'Dustimus Maximus' species, thriving on neglected bookshelves."

As he began to clean, RJ found himself assigning personalities to various objects around his apartment. The stubborn stain on the carpet became 'Spot,' a worthy adversary in an epic battle of man versus grime.

"We meet again, Spot," RJ growled, brandishing a spray bottle like a weapon. "You may have won the last round, but I've come prepared this time. Prepare to meet your maker... or at least, the washing machine!"

Hours passed, and RJ's apartment slowly transformed from "potential health hazard" to "almost presentable." Throughout the process, his self-talk had taken on the role of a motivational coach, cheerleader, and occasional drill sergeant:

"Come on, RJ! You're almost there! Just think of how good it'll feel to have a clean apartment. You might even find that fork you lost three weeks ago!"

"Ten-hut, soldier! I don't want to see a single dust bunny surviving this purge. Show no mercy!"

"And the crowd goes wild as RJ successfully navigates the obstacle course of dirty laundry without breaking his neck! What an athlete, ladies and gentlemen!"

By the time he finished, RJ was exhausted but oddly exhilarated. He'd never thought cleaning could be so... entertaining. As he collapsed onto his now-visible couch, he couldn't help but give himself a pat on the back:

"Well done, old chap! We make a pretty good team, don't we? Although, I have to say, your David Attenborough impression needs some work."

As RJ's self-talk habit grew, so did its complexity. He found himself engaging in full-blown internal debates, complete with different voices and personalities. This new development came in particularly handy during decision-making processes, like when RJ was trying to decide whether to attend his high school reunion:

Optimistic RJ: "Come on, it'll be fun! A chance to reconnect with old friends, see how everyone's doing."

Pessimistic RJ: "Are you kidding? It'll be a parade of awkward small talk and thinly veiled life comparisons. Hard pass."

Rational RJ: "Let's think about this logically. What are the potential benefits versus the drawbacks?"

Nostalgic RJ: "Remember prom night? The terrible haircuts? The crushes we never confessed?"

Anxious RJ: "Oh goodness, what if they remember that time we tripped during the school play and knocked over the entire set?"

As the debate raged on in his head, RJ found himself pacing back and forth in his living room, gesticulating wildly as each 'personality' made its case. It was only when he heard a knock at the door that he froze, realizing how this must look to an outside observer.

His neighbor, Mrs. Johnson, stood at the door with a concerned look on her face. "Is everything alright, dear? I heard voices and what sounded like an argument."

RJ's face flushed red as he scrambled for an explanation. "Oh, uh, yes! Everything's fine, Mrs. Johnson. I was just... rehearsing for a play! A one-man show about... a man with multiple personalities deciding whether to attend his high school reunion."

Mrs. Johnson's concern morphed into confusion, then polite interest. "Oh, how... avant-garde. Well, break a leg, dear. But do try to keep it down after 10, won't you?"

As he closed the door, RJ couldn't help but chuckle at the absurdity of the situation. "Well, RJ," he said to himself, "looks like we need to work on our indoor voices. Or invest in some seriously soundproof walls."

Despite the occasional embarrassing moment, RJ found that his evolving self-talk was becoming an invaluable tool in his daily life. It helped him process complex emotions, work through difficult decisions, and even served as a source of entertainment during mundane tasks.

One particularly stressful day at work, RJ found himself on the verge of a meltdown after a series of coding disasters. As he felt his anxiety rising, he took a deep breath and initiated an internal pep talk:

"Alright, RJ, let's take a step back here. Remember, you've faced worse challenges than this. Remember the Great Coffee Spill of 2018? You managed to save both your laptop and your dignity... well, mostly your laptop."

He couldn't help but smile at the memory, feeling his stress levels decrease slightly.

"That's it, deep breaths. You've got this. You're the Coding Ninja, the Debugging Dynamo, the... guy who really needs to cool it with the cheesy nicknames."

By the end of his internal monologue, RJ felt centered enough to tackle the problem with renewed focus. He realized that his self-talk had become more than just a quirky habit – it was a coping mechanism, a problem-solving tool, and sometimes, a much-needed friend.

As RJ's self-talk continued to evolve, he began to wonder about its implications. Was this normal? Was he tapping into some hidden potential of the human mind, or was he slowly losing his marbles? These questions led him to the next stage of his journey – seeking clarity and understanding about his chatty new relationship with himself.

But that, dear reader, is a story for our next section. For now, let's leave RJ as he ponders these questions, carrying on an animated discussion with himself about the nature of consciousness, blissfully unaware of the strange looks he's getting from passersby as he walks down the street, gesticulating wildly and occasionally bursting into laughter at his own jokes.

"Oh, RJ," he chuckled to himself, "life may be crazy, but at least it's never boring with you around."

Seeking Clarity: RJ's Response to His SelfTalk

As RJ's self-talk habit grew more pronounced, so did his curiosity about it. Was this normal? Was he onto something revolutionary, or was he one coffee away from starring in his own psychological thriller? It was time to seek some answers, and in true RJ fashion, he approached this quest for clarity with a mix of determination, humor, and only a slight fear that he might end up on some sort of watch list.

The Great Google Adventure

RJ's first stop on his journey to understanding was, naturally, Google. Armed with a fresh cup of coffee and a plate of cookies (brain food, he assured himself), he settled in for what he expected to be a quick search. Little did he know, he was about to fall down a rabbit hole that would make Alice's adventures in Wonderland look like a quick trip to the corner store.

"Okay, Google," RJ muttered, fingers poised over the keyboard. "Don't fail me now. 'Is talking to yourself normal?'"

Three hours and countless open tabs later, RJ emerged from his research haze, bleary-eyed and more confused than ever. He had somehow gone from articles about self-talk to conspiracy theories about sentient AI, with a brief detour through cat videos (how did that even happen?).

"Well," he said to his empty room, "that was about as helpful as a chocolate teapot. Though I did learn how to fold fitted sheets, so not a total loss."

The Library Escapade

Deciding that perhaps old-school research methods might yield better results, RJ headed to the local library. As he perused the psychology section, he couldn't help but provide his own running commentary:

"'Understanding the Voices in Your Head,'" RJ read aloud, then quickly glanced around to make sure no one had heard him. "Bit on the nose, don't you think? Maybe we should start with something a little less... incriminating."

As he reached for another book, he lost his balance on the small step ladder he was using. In a moment of panic, he grabbed the nearest shelf, sending a cascade of books raining down around him.

Sprawled on the floor, surrounded by a sea of psychology texts, RJ looked up to see the stern face of the librarian looming over him.

"I'm conducting a, uh, gravity experiment," he offered weakly. "You know, for science."

The librarian's expression didn't change as she handed him a broom and dustpan.

The Doctor's Visit

Realizing that perhaps he needed professional input, RJ decided to visit his family doctor. He spent the entire morning rehearsing how to broach the subject without sounding like he needed to be committed.

In the doctor's office, RJ fidgeted nervously. "So, Doc," he began, trying to sound casual, "hypothetically speaking, if someone were to talk to themselves... a lot... like, having full conversations and debates and maybe the occasional musical number... that would be totally normal, right?"

The doctor peered at him over her glasses. "Are we talking about you, RJ?"

"Me? Oh no, no," RJ laughed nervously. "It's for a friend. A very hypothetical friend who is definitely not me."

"Mm-hmm," the doctor nodded, clearly unconvinced. "And does this 'friend' hear voices telling him to do things?"

"What? No!" RJ exclaimed. "The voices- I mean, the hypothetical voices - are all him. Talking to himself. About normal things like coding, and groceries, and sometimes pretending to be a sports announcer during particularly intense sessions of solving Rubik's cubes."

The doctor's expression softened. "RJ, self-talk is quite common and often beneficial. It can help with problem-solving, reducing stress, and improving focus. However," she added, seeing RJ's relieved expression, "if it's interfering with your daily life or causing distress, we might want to discuss it further."

RJ left the doctor's office feeling both relieved and slightly embarrassed. As he walked to his car, he couldn't help but chuckle at himself.

"Well, RJ," he said, "Good news! We're not crazy. Eccentric, sure. Possibly in need of a hobby that doesn't involve talking to ourselves, maybe. But not crazy!"

The Friend Experiment

Emboldened by the doctor's reassurance, RJ decided to broach the subject with his friends. He invited a small group over for a game night, planning to casually bring up the topic of self-talk.

As they settled in to play Monopoly (a game that RJ felt might naturally lead to people talking to themselves in frustration), he tried to steer the conversation.

"So," he said, attempting nonchalance while distributing colorful money, "does anyone else ever, you know, talk to themselves?"

His friends exchanged glances.

"You mean like when you're trying to remember something?" one friend asked.

"Or when you stub your toe and curse at the furniture?" another chimed in.

"No, no," RJ pressed on. "I mean like full conversations. Debates. Maybe the occasional impersonation of David Attenborough narrating your life."

Silence fell over the room. RJ felt his face growing hot.

"Asking for a friend, of course," he added quickly.

To his surprise and relief, his friends burst out laughing.

"Oh, RJ," his best friend grinned, "only you would worry about this. Of course we all talk to ourselves. Maybe not with your... enthusiasm, but it's totally normal."

As the night wore on, RJ found himself regaling his friends with tales of his self-talk adventures, much to their amusement. By the end of the evening, they were all trying to out-do each other with their best David Attenborough impressions.

The Acceptance

As RJ lay in bed that night, reflecting on his journey for clarity, he felt a sense of peace wash over him. Sure, his self-talk might be a bit more elaborate than most, but it was part of what made him uniquely RJ.

"Well, old chap," he said to himself, snuggling into his pillow, "looks like you're stuck with me. But hey, at least life will never be boring."

With a chuckle and a yawn, RJ drifted off to sleep, his mind already buzzing with ideas for tomorrow's internal conversations. As he teetered on the edge of consciousness, he could have sworn he heard a voice that sounded suspiciously like Morgan Freeman say, "And so, RJ embraced his quirky habit, ready to face whatever adventures his chatty mind would lead him to next."

RJ smiled in his sleep. Life with self-talk might be weird, but it was certainly never dull.

Concluding Thoughts

As we wrap up this whirlwind tour of RJ's awakening to the world of self-talk, it's clear that our protagonist has embarked on a journey as entertaining as it is enlightening. From debugging code with theatrical flair to turning grocery shopping into a one-man sports commentary, RJ has transformed the mundane into the extraordinary, all through the power of talking to himself.

Let's take a moment to recap RJ's adventures in self-dialogue:

1. **The Accidental Beginning** : What started as a frustrated outburst at a stubborn piece of code blossomed into a fullfledged conversation with himself. Little did RJ know that this moment would be the first step on a path to self-discovery (and occasional public embarrassment).

1. **The Everyday Evolution** : RJ's self-talk quickly infiltrated every aspect of his life. Suddenly, brushing teeth became an Olympic event, and choosing cereal turned into an existential crisis. Who knew that the simple act of talking to oneself could turn life into an improv comedy show?

1. **The Complexity Conundrum** : As RJ's self-talk evolved, so did its intricacy. From simple mutterings to full-blown internal debates complete with different personas, RJ's mind became a veritable theater of the absurd. One can only imagine the chaos if he ever decided to write an autobiographical play.

1. **The Quest for Clarity** : In true RJ fashion, his search for understanding and personal mastery was as hilarious as it was earnest. From falling down internet rabbit holes to creating a book

avalanche in the library, RJ's journey to self-understanding was anything but boring. And let's not forget the doctor's visit that probably had his physician seriously considering a career change.

1. **The Social Experiment** : RJ's bravery in confiding in his friends not only brought relief but also sparked a David Attenborough impersonation contest. Who says self-talk can't be a group activity?

1. **The Acceptance** : Finally, RJ embraced his chatty nature, realizing that his internal dialogue was not a quirk to be cured but a unique part of his personality to be celebrated (and occasionally hushed in public spaces).

As we bid farewell to this chapter of RJ's life, we're left with the image of our hero, snuggled in bed, drifting off to sleep with a smile on his face and the voice of Morgan Freeman narrating in his head. It's a fitting end to a part of his journey that has been equal parts introspective and ridiculous.

But this is far from the end of RJ's story. Oh no, dear reader, we're just getting started. As RJ embraces his self-talk, new questions arise: How will this newfound self-awareness affect his daily life? What benefits might he discover? And most importantly, will he ever perfect his David Attenborough impression?

As we look ahead to Part II: The Benefits, we can only imagine the adventures that await our intrepid self-talker. Will RJ use his internal dialogue to become a productivity powerhouse? Might he develop a new problem-solving technique that revolutionizes the tech industry?

Or will he simply find new and inventive ways to entertain himself during mundane tasks?

One thing's for certain: with RJ's penchant for turning everyday situations into comedic gold, we're in for a treat. So grab your metaphorical popcorn, settle in, and prepare for more laugh-outloud moments as we continue to explore the weird and wonderful world of RJ's self-talk.

Remember, in the words of RJ himself: "Life might be crazy, but at least it's never boring when you're your own best conversation partner!"

Part II: The Benefits

Effective Self-Talk for Personal Development

As RJ continued his journey into the world of self-talk, he began to realize that his chatty habit was more than just an entertaining quirk. It was like discovering that his childhood imaginary friend had grown up to become a life coach, therapist, and personal cheerleader all rolled into one. Let's dive into the treasure trove of benefits RJ uncovered, shall we?

Clarity of Thought: How self-talk helps RJ organize ideas

RJ's mind had always been a bit like a teenager's bedroom – cluttered, chaotic, and occasionally harboring something that might have once been a sandwich. But with self-talk, he found a way to tidy up this mental mess.

One morning, as RJ prepared for a crucial meeting at work, his thoughts were particularly jumbled:

"Okay, focus RJ. We need to prepare for the meeting, feed Simon the cockatiel, remember to buy milk, and figure out why the neighbor's cat keeps staring at me through the window. Is it judging my coding skills? Can cats even code?"

Realizing he was getting off track, RJ took a deep breath and started talking to himself more deliberately:

"Alright, let's break this down. First things first – the meeting. What are the key points we need to cover?"

As he verbalized his thoughts, RJ found himself mentally organizing his ideas, like a master chef separating ingredients for a complex recipe.

"Point one: Project timeline. Point two: Budget concerns. Point three: That weird bug that makes the program play 'Never Gonna Give You Up' every time someone types the word 'pickle'."

By the time RJ had finished his self-talk session, he had a clear, organized plan for the meeting. As an added bonus, he'd also remembered to add milk to his shopping list and decided that the neighbor's cat was probably just admiring his impressive collection of Star Wars figurines visible through the window.

This newfound clarity extended to other areas of RJ's life as well. Grocery shopping, once a labyrinthine ordeal, became a wellexecuted mission:

"Alright, RJ, let's approach this systematically. Produce first – we need lettuce, tomatoes, and those weird kiwis that look like tiny Chewbaccas. Then to dairy – milk, eggs, and that fancy cheese you can't pronounce but pretend to know about at parties. Finally, the snack aisle – but remember, we're only getting one type of chip. We don't need a repeat of the Great Chip Fiasco of 2022."

As he navigated the store, RJ couldn't help but feel a sense of accomplishment. "Look at us," he muttered proudly while examining avocados, "adulting like a boss. Marie Kondo would be proud."

Problem-Solving Partner: RJ using self-talk to work through challenge

RJ soon discovered that his inner voice was not just a chatterbox but also an excellent problem-solving partner. It was like having a personal assistant, life coach, and occasional comedian all rolled into one.

One weekend, RJ found himself facing a particularly daunting challenge: assembling a piece of furniture with instructions that seemed to be written in an alien language.

"Okay, RJ," he said, staring at the sea of wooden panels and mysterious screws spread across his living room floor. "We've written complex algorithms. We've debugged impossible errors. Surely, we can conquer this... whatever this is supposed to be."

As he worked through the process, RJ's self-talk became a running commentary:

"Insert tab A into slot B. Right. But which one is tab A? Is it this long pointy bit? Or this thing that looks like it could be a modern art masterpiece?"

After several attempts and a few choice words muttered under his breath, RJ decided to change his approach:

"Let's think about this logically. If we were designing this furniture, how would we want it assembled? Imagine we're writing a program, but instead of code, we're using wood and screws."

This shift in perspective, facilitated by his self-talk, helped RJ see the problem in a new light. He began to approach the assembly like a coding problem, breaking it down into smaller, manageable steps.

"First, we group similar pieces. Then, we identify the main structure. After that, we attach the smaller elements. It's just like building a program's architecture!"

Three hours, two minor injuries, and one nearly swallowed screw later, RJ stood back to admire his handiwork. The furniture piece stood proudly (if slightly lopsided) in his living room.

"We did it!" RJ exclaimed, high-fiving himself. "Take that, indecipherable instructions! RJ: 1, Alien Furniture Overlords: 0!"

This problem-solving prowess began to spill over into RJ's work life as well. Debugging became less of a chore and more of an entertaining detective novel:

"Elementary, my dear RJ," he'd say in his best Sherlock Holmes impression, scrutinizing a particularly tricky piece of code. "The culprit must be hiding in this function. But what's its motive? Why would it choose to crash the system every time someone clicks the 'Save' button while holding their breath and standing on one foot?"

Colleagues started to notice RJ's improved problem-solving skills, though they were slightly puzzled by his tendency to shout "Eureka!" and do a victory dance every time he fixed a bug.

As RJ continued to explore the power of self-talk, he found it particularly useful in managing his emotions and staying motivated. His inner voice became a personal cheerleader, therapist, and occasional drill sergeant.

One morning, RJ woke up feeling particularly unmotivated. The thought of tackling his to-do list seemed as appealing as debugging an entire program written in emoji code.

"I can't do this," he groaned into his pillow. "Maybe if I just lie here, the world will forget about me, and I won't have to adult today."

But then, another part of him chimed in:

"Come on! Are you really going to let a little case of the Mondays defeat you? You're the guy who once stayed up for 48 hours straight to finish a project fueled by nothing but coffee and sheer determination!"

RJ couldn't help but smile at the memory. "That's true," he admitted to himself. "Though I'm pretty sure I hallucinated that my computer was talking to me towards the end there."

"See? If you can survive that, you can handle anything! Now, let's break this day down into small, manageable tasks. First step: get out of bed without injuring yourself."

With a chuckle, RJ swung his legs over the side of the bed, narrowly avoiding tripping over a stray shoe.

"Step one: accomplished! Look at you, already succeeding at life!" Throughout the day, RJ continued to use self-talk to regulate his emotions and stay motivated. When faced with a particularly challenging task, he'd give himself a pep talk:

"Alright, RJ, this is tough, but so are you. Remember the time you explained coding to your grandma and she actually understood it? If you can do that, you can do anything!"

By the end of the day, RJ had not only completed his to-do list but had also managed to stay positive and motivated throughout. As he settled in for the evening, he couldn't help but give himself one last pat on the back:

"Well done, old chap! We make a pretty good team, don't we? Me, myself, and I – the dream team of productivity!"

As the weeks went by, RJ's colleagues noticed a change in him. He seemed more resilient in the face of challenges, bouncing back from setbacks with a determination that bordered on superhuman (or at least super-caffeinated).

Little did they know that behind RJ's newfound emotional stability was a constant stream of internal pep talks, dad jokes, and the occasional imaginary dance-off between his motivated self and his procrastinating self. (Motivated RJ always won, mainly because Procrastinating RJ kept putting off learning the dance moves.)

In the end, RJ realized that the greatest benefit of his self-talk wasn't just improved clarity, problem-solving, or emotional regulation. It was the fact that he'd become his own best friend, supporter, and source of entertainment. Life might throw its challenges, but with his trusty inner voice by his side, RJ felt ready to face anything – even if it meant occasionally looking like he was arguing with thin air in public.

As he drifted off to sleep that night, a smile played on RJ's lips. "You know what, RJ?" he mumbled to himself, "I think this is the beginning of a beautiful friendship."

And with that, RJ fell asleep, his mind already buzzing with ideas for tomorrow's internal adventures. Who knew what problems he'd solve, what emotions he'd navigate, or what imaginary acceptance speeches he'd practice in the shower? One thing was for sure – life with self-talk was never, ever boring.

Clarity of Thought: How self-talk helps RJ organize ideas

When RJ first began practicing self-talk, he was astounded by how it instantly turned the chaos in his mind into a well-organized flow of thoughts. Imagine, for example, trying to juggle multiple tasks at work while also remembering to buy groceries and plan for a weekend trip. Without self-talk, these tasks would resemble a tornado swirling inside RJ's head, creating confusion and stress. Through self-talk, RJ found a way to break down complex ideas into manageable parts, separating each task into digestible segments.

This process is almost like having a personal assistant in your brain, making mental checklists - imagine if we could use AI and chip implants with special code? By asking himself questions ("What should I tackle first?" or "Which task has the earliest deadline?"), RJ can prioritize effectively. Pausing to engage in this internal dialogue, he realizes that not all tasks have equal importance or urgency. Selftalk encourages him to focus on what truly matters, enabling him to schedule his time wisely and avoid last-minute panics.

Take a typical Monday morning when RJ's boss throws an unexpected project his way. Initially, the sheer scope of the project might seem overwhelming. With self-talk, RJ is able to mentally outline the main components: research, strategy, execution, and review. He then breaks each component into smaller tasks such as gathering information, drafting plans, and setting deadlines. This division makes the large project appear less intimidating, allowing RJ to start working without feeling paralyzed by its enormity.

Next, let's consider the confidence boost RJ gets from self-talk. Internal dialogue allows RJ to reflect on past experiences, turning them into valuable lessons for the future. When faced with tough decisions, RJ often recalls similar situations he navigated successfully. For instance, if he once solved a tight deadline issue by delegating tasks efficiently, he reminds himself of that success through self-talk. This reflection bolsters his confidence and helps him make informed decisions based on past achievements and mistakes.

Self-talk doesn't just dwell on the past; it actively involves RJ in problem-solving by identifying gaps in his understanding. Suppose RJ encounters a snag in his current project because he lacks specific information. Instead of spiraling into frustration, he asks himself targeted questions: "What aspects am I missing?" or "Who can I reach out to for help?" This verbalization sharpens his awareness, leading him to pinpoint precisely what's required to bridge those gaps and seek solutions effectively.

Moreover, RJ finds that by voicing his thoughts internally, he gains clarity and insight quicker than through passive thinking. It's as if speaking—or thinking—aloud brings hidden thoughts to the forefront, making them easier to analyze. This approach is akin to writing notes during a meeting; putting thoughts into words transforms abstract concepts into concrete steps.

It's essential to underline that RJ's internal conversations are not stiff monologues but dynamic dialogues. They're filled with curiosity, humor, and even a bit of self-criticism. Sometimes, RJ pretends he's giving advice to a friend, which often leads to more compassionate and constructive self-talk. On occasions, this inner monologue morphs into pep talks, especially when he's on the verge of procrastination. Phrases like "Just start somewhere" or "Let's just dive in for ten minutes" have become his go-to mantras, pushing him into action.

To visualize this, picture RJ deliberating over whether to commence a particularly daunting report. His brain prefers the comfort of browsing social media or diving into simpler tasks. However, using self-talk, RJ convinces himself with gentle yet firm prompts. A mental nudge saying, "The sooner we start, the sooner it's done," or "How about we just outline the main points?" frequently turns hesitation into productivity.

RJ's case isn't unique. Many people find their productivity skyrockets through effective self-talk. It doesn't require special skills or tools; it's merely a habit of engaging in purposeful conversation with oneself. When done consistently, it acts as a strong foundation for mental organization, boosting both efficiency and confidence.

Problem-Solving Partner: RJ using self-talk to work through challenges

Navigating the maze of life's obstacles can sometimes feel like an impossible task. However, RJ has discovered a powerful tool that helps him stay on track: self-talk. By engaging in internal dialogue, he is able to brainstorm multiple solutions to a single problem, weigh the pros and cons of each approach, anticipate potential setbacks, and maintain emotional clarity.

When RJ encounters a tricky situation, his first step is to engage in self-talk to explore various possibilities. Whether it's a work-related issue or a personal dilemma, RJ's internal monologue becomes his brainstorming session. For example, if he's faced with a tight deadline at work, he might start by listing out possible actions: delegating tasks, prioritizing the most urgent assignments, or even negotiating for an extension. This initial phase of brainstorming allows RJ to open up his mind and consider all angles, from the obvious to the creative.

After generating a list of potential solutions, RJ uses self-talk to evaluate each option systematically. He weighs the pros and cons, asking himself questions like, "If I delegate this task, will it be done to my standards?" or "What are the risks if I ask for more time?" It's like having a mini-debate in his own head, where he plays the roles of both the optimist and the skeptic. This process not only helps RJ in refining his options but also gives him the confidence to proceed with the most viable solution.

One of the key advantages of self-talk is its ability to help RJ foresee potential setbacks. By going through different scenarios in his mind, RJ can identify possible hurdles and prepare contingency plans accordingly. Imagine RJ planning a big presentation. Through selftalk, he anticipates technical difficulties, challenging questions from the audience, and even his own nerves acting up. As a result, he makes sure to have backup slides, rehearses answers to expected tough questions, and practices calming techniques. By being proactive, RJ ensures he's ready for whatever comes his way.

Guidelines are particularly useful when seeking to manage one's emotions effectively. RJ finds that self-talk is instrumental in keeping his cool in stressful situations. When his stress levels rise, he turns inward and talks himself through the anxiety. He reminds himself to breathe deeply, focus on the present moment, and take one step at a time. This simple act of speaking kindly to oneself can profoundly impact emotional regulation. By repeating affirmations like, "I've handled worse before," or "I am capable and prepared," RJ can transform his nervous energy into focused determination.

An incident at work vividly illustrates how self-talk aids RJ in maintaining composure. During a critical meeting, RJ was unexpectedly asked to explain a project detail he hadn't prepared for. Instead of panicking, he quickly engaged in self-talk: "Stay calm. Think about what you know. You got this." This internal pep talk enabled RJ to collect his thoughts and respond coherently, impressing his colleagues with his poise under pressure.

Moreover, RJ's practice of self-talk doesn't just stop at managing immediate obstacles; it extends into future preparedness. Having successfully navigated one challenge through self-talk, RJ often reflects on the experience to refine his strategies. He asks himself questions like, "What went well?" and "What could I improve next time?" This continual loop of analysis and reflection helps him grow more resilient and adaptable.

RJ's habit of using self-talk as a motivational tool shouldn't be underestimated either. When facing mundane tasks or long-term projects, he engages in a supportive dialogue with himself to stay motivated. He breaks down larger goals into smaller, manageable steps and celebrates small victories along the way. Statements such as "Completing this part today gets me closer to my end goal" keep RJ energized and focused. Even on days when motivation wanes, positive self-talk acts as a steady anchor, reminding him of the bigger picture.

In essence, RJ's use of self-talk encapsulates a holistic approach to overcoming life's hurdles. From brainstorming and evaluating solutions to preparing for setbacks and regulating emotions, selftalk serves as a versatile tool in his personal development arsenal. By consistently practicing this internal dialogue, RJ not only tackles challenges effectively but also enhances his mental resilience and clarity.

Emotional Regulation and Motivation: RJ calming and encouraging himself through internal dialogue

When RJ finds himself overwhelmed with stress, he ignites the power of internal dialogue. By engaging in an honest conversation with himself, he gains a valuable outlet to vent and process his emotions. Picture RJ after a long day at work: deadlines looming, emails piling up, and that stubborn printer refusing to cooperate.

Instead of bottling up his frustrations, RJ takes a moment to step aside and have a candid chat with himself. "Alright, RJ," he might say, "this day has been a rollercoaster, but you're doing your best. Let's figure out how to handle this." This seemingly simple act allows him to acknowledge his feelings and find clarity amid the chaos.

In these internal conversations, RJ also incorporates positive affirmations to boost his confidence. Imagine RJ preparing for a big presentation. The butterflies in his stomach are fluttering non-stop. He stands in front of a mirror and says, "You've got this, RJ. You've done this before, and you'll do it again. You are prepared, confident, and capable." These affirmations serve as powerful reminders of his strengths and abilities. Over time, they become embedded in his mindset, transforming his inner critic into his biggest supporter. Every time doubt creeps in, RJ counters it with a positive affirmation, reinforcing his self-belief.

Setting realistic goals is another crucial way RJ uses self-talk for personal development. When feeling ambitious, RJ doesn't just aimlessly declare lofty aspirations. He sits down with himself and thoughtfully outlines achievable steps. "Okay, RJ," he might muse, "you want to run a marathon. Let's break it down. First, we'll start by running a mile every day. Then, we'll gradually increase the distance." By talking through his plans, RJ ensures that his goals are not only ambitious but also attainable. This methodical approach prevents him from feeling overwhelmed and encourages steady progress.

Another vital aspect of self-talk is reminding oneself of past achievements, which RJ frequently does. Whenever doubt threatens to derail him, he reflects on previous successes. "Remember when you aced that project last year? It took hard work and dedication, but you pulled it off. You can do it again." These reflections reinforce RJ's sense of capability and resilience. By recalling concrete examples of his accomplishments, he builds a reservoir of motivation to draw upon in challenging times. This practice isn't about living in the past but rather using past victories to propel future endeavors.

Self-coaching is where RJ truly shines. He becomes his own cheerleader, especially when the going gets tough. During those moments when everything seems to go wrong – the car breaks down, the assignment is overdue, and the flu strikes – RJ doesn't wallow in self-pity. Instead, he gives himself a pep talk. "Alright, RJ, this is tough, but you're tougher. Take a deep breath, prioritize what needs to be done, and tackle each task one at a time. You've faced worse and come out stronger."

To make self-coaching effective, one could follow RJ's guideline:

1. **Acknowledge the Situation** : Begin by recognizing the challenge without sugarcoating it. See it for what it really is.

2. **Reaffirm Self-Worth** : Remind yourself of your strengths and past successes.

3. **Break Down the Problem** : Tackle the issue step by step, focusing on manageable tasks. Don't start it all on day one!

4. **Stay Positive** : Maintain a positive outlook, even if progress is slow. Ups and Downs are cycles found everywhere. Learn to live with the ups and downs of life!

By following this structured approach, RJ maintains his motivation and perseverance. He doesn't allow setbacks to dictate his actions. Instead, he views them as opportunities to coach himself through adversity.

An integral part of RJ's self-talk routine involves regular check-ins with his emotional state. Throughout the day, RJ assesses how he feels and addresses any negative emotions head-on. If he notices he's becoming anxious, he might pause and say, "RJ, let's take a moment to breathe. What's causing this anxiety, and how can we manage it?" These frequent self-assessments help him stay attuned to his emotional needs, ensuring he remains balanced and focused.

Balancing self-talk with action is crucial. RJ knows that while selftalk is a powerful tool, it must be accompanied by actionable steps. After bolstering his confidence and setting clear goals, RJ doesn't just sit back. He actively works towards his objectives, using his selftalk as a foundation for his efforts. This balance between internal dialogue and external action is key to his personal development.

Enhanced Creativity: RJ's Imaginative Breakthroughs

As RJ continued to embrace his self-talk habit, he stumbled upon an unexpected benefit: a significant boost in creativity. It was as if his inner dialogue had opened a secret door in his mind, leading to a room full of wild ideas and imaginative solutions.

One day, while working on a particularly challenging coding project, RJ found himself stuck. The problem seemed insurmountable, like trying to teach a cat to bark. Frustrated, he leaned back in his chair and began his usual self-talk:

"Alright, RJ, think outside the box. If this code were a pizza, how would you slice it?"

To his surprise, this absurd question sparked a series of equally absurd – but surprisingly insightful – thoughts:

"Well, if it were a pizza, I'd want it to be easily shareable. Maybe we can break this code into smaller, modular pieces? And just like you can customize toppings, we could make these modules customizable for different use cases!"

Before he knew it, RJ was scribbling diagrams of pizza-inspired code architecture on his whiteboard. His colleagues walked by, giving him strange looks as he muttered about "pepperoni functions" and "cheese string theory," but RJ was too engrossed in his creative breakthrough to notice.

This newfound creativity spilled over into other areas of RJ's life. Cooking, once a utilitarian task, became an adventure in culinary innovation:

"What if we combined spaghetti with tacos?" RJ mused aloud while staring into his fridge. "We could call it... Spaghetticos! Or maybe Tacghetti?"

While his creations didn't always turn out as planned (the Great Sushi Burrito Incident of 2023 was particularly memorable), RJ found joy in the process of ideation and experimentation.

Improved Decision Making: RJ's Internal Debate Club

Another unexpected benefit of RJ's self-talk was a marked improvement in his decision-making skills. It was as if he had internalized an entire debate club, ready to argue the pros and cons of every choice.

When faced with the decision of whether to accept a new job offer, RJ's internal dialogue kicked into high gear:

"Okay, let's break this down," he said, pacing his living room. "Pro: Higher salary. Con: Longer commute. Pro: More challenging work. Con: Less time for our vital Netflix binge-watching sessions."

As he verbalized each point, RJ found himself considering angles he might have otherwise overlooked. He even assigned different voices to different perspectives:

"But think of the career growth!" argued Ambitious RJ in a booming voice.

"What about work-life balance?" countered Laid-back RJ, sounding suspiciously like Jeff Bridges in "The Big Lebowski."

"Have we considered the snack situation in the new office?" chimed in Hungry RJ, because priorities.

By the end of his internal debate, RJ had a comprehensive pros and cons list and a much clearer perspective on the decision. Plus, he'd managed to entertain his neighbor's cat, who had been watching the entire performance through the window with a mixture of confusion and judgment.

Stress Reduction: RJ's Self-Soothing Techniques

As RJ became more adept at self-talk, he discovered its powerful ability to reduce stress. It was like having a personal stress ball that could talk back and occasionally tell jokes.

During particularly hectic periods at work, RJ developed a habit of giving himself pep talks:

"You've got this, RJ," he'd mutter while tackling a mountain of tasks. "You're a coding ninja, a debugging samurai, a... guy who really needs to cool it with the warrior metaphors."

These self-affirming statements, often delivered with a healthy dose of self-deprecating humor, helped RJ maintain his cool under pressure.

His colleagues marveled at his newfound zen, unaware that beneath his calm exterior was a constant stream of internal cheerleading and occasional imaginary dance-offs.

RJ even developed a technique he called "Debugging Life," where he approached personal problems like he would a stubborn piece of code:

"Error: Kitchen sink clogged. Possible causes: 1) Food debris, 2) Small kitchen utensils, 3) Portal to another dimension. Solutions: 1) Plunger, 2) Drain snake, 3) Contact Dr. Strange."

While this approach didn't always solve the problem, it invariably made RJ chuckle, reducing his stress and putting him in a better mindset to tackle the issue.

Enhanced Learning: RJ's Self-Taught Teaching Method

RJ soon realized that self-talk was an incredible tool for learning and retaining new information. It was like having a study buddy available 24/7, albeit one with an uncanny resemblance to himself.

When learning a new programming language, RJ took to explaining concepts out loud as if teaching an invisible student:

"Now, pay attention, class," he'd say to his empty living room, adjusting an imaginary pair of glasses. "In Python, indentation is crucial. It's not just about looking pretty – although, let's face it, well-indented code is the supermodel of the programming world."

This method not only helped RJ grasp complex concepts more quickly but also led to some amusing situations. Like the time he was so engrossed in explaining object-oriented programming to his "class" that he didn't notice his video call with actual colleagues had started. His team was treated to a solid minute of RJ dramatically acting out the lifecycle of an object, complete with different voices for the constructor, methods, and destructor.

After the initial embarrassment wore off, RJ's unique teaching style became legendary in the office. Soon, junior developers were asking for the "RJ Special" – a explanation that was equal parts informative and entertaining, with a side of borderline ridiculous metaphors.

Improved Social Skills: RJ's Conversation Rehearsals

Surprisingly, RJ's habit of talking to himself actually improved his social skills. By rehearsing conversations and scenarios in his head, he became more confident and articulate in real-life social situations.

Before attending networking events, RJ would practice his small talk:

"So, what do you do?" he'd ask his reflection in the mirror. "Oh, me? I wrangle semicolons and herd unruly bits of code into submission. It's like being a digital cowboy, but with less horses and more coffee."

These rehearsals helped RJ feel more prepared and less anxious in social settings. However, they also led to some amusing mix-ups, like the time he accidentally used one of his rehearsed jokes on his dentist:

"What's a programmer's favorite place to hang out? The Foo Bar!"

The confused silence that followed was broken only by the sound of the dental suction tube.

Despite occasional misfires, RJ's improved social skills and quick wit made him a hit at office parties. Little did his colleagues know that behind every smooth interaction was hours of self-talk practice and an internal cheer squad rooting him on.

As RJ continued to discover new benefits to his self-talk habit, he couldn't help but marvel at how this quirky trait had transformed his life. Sure, he might occasionally get odd looks when caught midconversation with himself at the supermarket, but the pros far outweighed the cons.

"You know what, RJ?" he said to himself one evening, relaxing after a particularly productive day. "I think we've stumbled onto something pretty amazing here. Who knew talking to yourself could be a superpower?"

With a contented sigh, RJ settled in for a night of surfing High Definiton Television Channels, already looking forward to tomorrow's adventures in self-talk. After all, life is always interesting when your best friend, life coach, and comedy partner lives right inside your head.

Bringing It All Together

In Part II, we've delved into the incredible power of self-talk and how it assists RJ in various facets of life. From organizing chaotic thoughts to solving complex problems and regulating emotions, RJ's internal dialogue transforms his daily challenges into manageable tasks. By breaking down large projects, reflecting on past successes, and brainstorming solutions, RJ not only stays organized but also boosts his confidence and keeps his stress levels in check. This practice of talking to himself has become an indispensable tool, helping him juggle multiple responsibilities with ease and turning potential panic into productive action.

Furthermore, RJ's self-talk is a dynamic blend of humor, curiosity, and positivity that keeps him motivated and emotionally balanced. Whether he's calming his nerves before a big presentation or pushing through mundane tasks, these internal pep talks keep him focused and resilient. The chapter shows us that anyone can harness this skill without needing special tools or training. All it takes is the habit of engaging in purposeful conversation with oneself, making self-talk a cornerstone for mental clarity, problem-solving, emotional regulation, and ongoing motivation.

Part III: The Pitfalls

Managing Internal Dialogue: RJ's Journey

Managing internal dialogue can feel like trying to tame a wild monkey with a megaphone. RJ's inner voice often swings from one random thought to another, leaving him exhausted and unsure of himself. Picture him walking down the street, dodging imaginary tomatoes thrown by an unseen audience judging his every move. The relentless chatter isn't just annoying; it's downright debilitating. By having meaningful conversations with ourselves instead of letting runaway thoughts dominate, we can begin building a healthier mental landscape. It's about transforming that inner critic into a more supportive and constructive presence.

In part III, we'll dive into the intricacies of RJ's internal dialogue, focusing on how significantly societal judgments can impact selfesteem and mental well-being. We'll explore strategies such as challenging societal misconceptions, surrounding oneself with positive influences, and finding a supportive community to buffer against negativity. Expect to uncover practical tools for building resilience, like practicing self-compassion and mindfulness, all aimed at turning RJ's critical monologue into a balanced conversation. Buckle up for a journey through managing internal dialogue, where the ultimate goal is not just surviving but thriving amid the mental noise.

Social Settings: RJ dealing with others

As RJ continued to embrace his chatty relationship with himself, he began to realize that, like any good friendship, it came with its own set of challenges. It turns out that having a constant conversation partner in your head isn't always smooth sailing. Let's dive into RJ's adventures as he navigates the pitfalls of his newfound habit.

RJ's first major hurdle came in the form of social stigma. While he had grown comfortable with his internal dialogue, the rest of the world wasn't always on the same page. This led to some... interesting situations.

Take, for instance, the Great Grocery Store Incident of 2023. RJ was in the produce section, engaged in an intense debate with himself about the merits of kale versus spinach:

"Sure, kale is trendy," he muttered, weighing a bunch in his hand, "but is it really worth the effort? It's like chewing on a healthconscious dinosaur's bathmat."

"But think of the nutrients!" his health-conscious inner voice argued back. "Plus, it makes you feel smugly superior at dinner parties."

As RJ continued his verbal pros and cons list, he failed to notice the growing audience of bemused shoppers around him. It wasn't until he turned to place the kale in his cart and came face-to-face with a wide-eyed child that he realized he'd been putting on quite the show.

"Mommy," the child stage-whispered, tugging on his mother's sleeve, "is that man friends with the vegetables?"

Red-faced and fumbling for an explanation, RJ managed to stammer out, "I'm, uh, practicing for a... one-man play. About the inner turmoil of produce selection."

As he hurriedly pushed his cart towards the checkout, leaving behind a wake of confused shoppers, RJ made a mental note: "Maybe tone down the veggie ventriloquism in public, old chap."

But the social awkwardness didn't stop there. RJ's habit of talking to himself began to affect his work life as well. During one particularly engaging internal dialogue about code optimization, RJ failed to notice that he had an audience:

"No, no, no," he muttered, gesticulating at his computer screen. "If we move this function here, it'll be more efficient. But wait, what about readability? Hmm, decisions, decisions..."

"Uh, RJ?" a voice interrupted his musings. RJ spun around to find his entire team standing in the doorway of his office, a mix of concern and amusement on their faces.

"Oh, hello!" RJ said, trying to act casual. "I was just... rubber duck debugging! You know how it is. Sometimes you just need to talk things out with an inanimate object. Or, in this case, an invisible rubber duck. With a British accent. Who's very opinionated about code structure."

His colleagues exchanged glances, clearly unsure whether to be impressed by his dedication or concerned for his sanity. From that day on, RJ noticed a marked increase in "wellness check" emails from HR.

As RJ became more comfortable with his internal dialogue, he found himself facing a new challenge: overthinking. It turned out that having a 24/7 conversation partner in your head could sometimes lead to mental roundabouts that were hard to exit.

One night, as RJ lay in bed trying to sleep, his mind began to wander:

"Did I remember to send that email to the client? Yes, I'm sure I did. Wait, did I? Maybe I should check. No, it's 2 AM, checking now would be ridiculous. But what if I forgot and the whole project falls apart and I get fired and end up living in a cardboard box talking to actual rubber ducks instead of imaginary ones?"

Before he knew it, RJ had spiraled into an epic internal debate about the butterfly effect of unsent emails, complete with imaginary scenarios and dramatic reenactments in his head. By the time his alarm went off the next morning, he had mentally scripted an entire movie trilogy about the perils of poor communication in the digital age.

Bleary-eyed and over-caffeinated, RJ stumbled into work, only to find that yes, he had indeed sent the email. As he slumped in his chair, relief warring with exhaustion, he couldn't help but chuckle at the absurdity of it all.

"Well, RJ," he muttered to himself, "looks like we need to work on an off switch for this overactive imagination of ours. Or at least invest in some industrial-strength melatonin."

As RJ continued his self-talk journey, he encountered perhaps the trickiest pitfall of all: the tendency for his inner voice to turn into a harsh critic. It was as if his internal dialogue had decided to channel Simon Cowell on a bad day.

One day, after a minor coding error led to a brief system crash, RJ found himself spiraling into a vortex of self-criticism:

"Way to go, genius," his inner voice sneered. "You had one job. ONE JOB. And you messed it up. You're about as useful as a chocolate teapot in a sauna."

RJ tried to shake off the negative thoughts, but they persisted, growing more creative (and ridiculous) in their criticism:

"If programming skills were currency, you'd be in debt. If they were a language, you'd be speaking in interpretive dance. If they were a superhero, you'd be Captain Keyboard-Smasher, defender of nothing and menace to functioning code everywhere!"

It wasn't until RJ caught sight of his reflection in his computer screen, looking dejected and hunched over his keyboard, that he realized how much this negative self-talk was affecting him.

"Alright, that's enough," he said firmly, straightening up in his chair. "We need to have a talk, me."

And so began the strangest intervention ever held – RJ staging an intervention for himself, with himself, by himself. He paced his office, alternating between the voice of reason and the overly critical voice:

Rational RJ: "Now, see here. Everyone makes mistakes. It's part of being human."

Critical RJ: "But not everyone crashes the system with a misplaced semicolon!"

Rational RJ: "It was quickly fixed, and no lasting damage was done. Plus, you learned from it."

Critical RJ: "Learned what? That I should pursue a career as a professional system crasher?"

Rational RJ: "Enough! We're better than this. From now on, for every negative thought, we have to come up with two positive ones. Deal?"

Critical RJ: (grumbling) "Fine. But I reserve the right to make sarcastic comments during code reviews."

Rational RJ: "Wouldn't have it any other way, old chap."

From that day forward, RJ worked on balancing his self-talk, turning his inner critic into more of a constructive feedback partner than a full-time heckler. It wasn't always easy, and there were days when the snarky comments slipped through, but overall, RJ found himself in a much healthier dialogue with himself.

As RJ's self-talk habit grew, he found himself facing an unexpected challenge: distraction. His inner voice, once a helpful companion, had developed a tendency to pipe up at the most inopportune moments, like a toddler who's just discovered the joy of interrupting adult conversations.

During one crucial meeting with a client, RJ found his mind wandering:

Client: "So, what do you think about implementing a new database structure?"

RJ's Inner Voice: "Oh, databases! Remember that time you accidentally deleted an entire table and had to reconstruct it from memory? Good times. Hey, speaking of memory, did you remember to buy cat food? We don't even have a cat. Why would we need cat food?"

RJ: (out loud, before he could stop himself) "Cat food database!"

The client stared at him, bewildered. RJ's colleagues shifted uncomfortably in their seats.

RJ: (attempting to recover) "I mean, uh, we should approach this database restructure as efficiently as a cat. You know, agile, flexible, always landing on our feet?"

As the meeting continued, RJ made a mental note to work on corralling his wandering thoughts. It was becoming clear that his inner voice needed some training in the art of time and place.

This tendency to get distracted by his own thoughts began to affect other areas of RJ's life as well. Simple tasks like doing laundry turned into epic mental odysseys:

RJ: (sorting laundry) "Okay, whites in this pile, colors in that one."

Inner Voice: "You know, the concept of separating whites and colors has some loaded historical connotations. Hey, that reminds me of that documentary we watched last week. Speaking of which, isn't it weird how we always say 'last week' even when it might have been 10 days ago? Who decided a week was seven days anyway? Was there a big meeting of ancient timekeepers?"

Before RJ knew it, he'd spent an hour pondering the sociopolitical implications of laundry and the arbitrary nature of time measurement, all while standing in front of the washing machine holding a single sock.

As these incidents piled up, RJ realized he needed to find a balance between engaging with his inner dialogue and staying focused on the task at hand. It was time to teach his inner voice the value of timing and relevance.

"Alright, chatty brain," RJ said to himself one evening, "we need to establish some ground rules. How about we save the philosophical debates and random trivia for designated times? Like shower thoughts, but more... scheduled."

And so, RJ began setting aside specific times for free-form internal discussions, like during his morning jog or while doing dishes. He also started practicing mindfulness techniques to help him stay present during important tasks.

It wasn't a perfect system – his inner voice still occasionally chimed in with ill-timed observations or random facts. But over time, RJ got better at gently steering his thoughts back on track.

"You know," RJ mused to himself one day, successfully folding laundry without pondering the meaning of life, "we make a pretty good team when we're not driving each other to distraction."

His inner voice, for once, simply agreed.

As RJ navigated these pitfalls, he realized that managing his internal dialogue was an ongoing process. It was a delicate balance between harnessing the benefits of self-talk and avoiding its potential drawbacks. But with each challenge he faced, RJ grew more adept at steering his inner conversations in a positive, productive direction.

Sure, there were still moments when he'd catch himself debating the merits of various pizza toppings in the middle of a code review, or rehearsing acceptance speeches for awards he hadn't won (and that didn't exist) while in line at the grocery store. But overall, RJ was learning to embrace his chatty nature while keeping it in check.

As he reflected on his journey so far, RJ couldn't help but chuckle. "Well, old chap," he said to himself, "life sure is interesting when your best friend, worst critic, and comedy partner all live in your head. Here's to many more adventures in the wild world of selftalk!"

And with that, RJ turned his attention back to his computer, ready to face whatever challenges – both external and internal – lay ahead.

After all, with a mind as active as his, boredom was never an option.

Social Stigma: RJ dealing with others' perceptions

Let's dive into RJ's journey of managing internal dialogue, especially focusing on the impact of social stigma. Picture this: RJ is walking down the street, and he can almost hear the whispers and feel the judgmental stares burning holes through his back. It's as if society has decided to become a panel of judges in a reality show, critiquing every step he makes. Social stigma can be an invisible weight that presses down on one's self-esteem like a ten-ton anchor.

Understanding how societal judgments affect self-esteem is crucial. Imagine you're carrying around a mirror all day, but instead of reflecting your true self, it reflects what others think of you. This distorted reflection can have a profound impact on how you perceive yourself. Research shows that constant negative feedback from society can lead to feelings of inadequacy and low self-worth. RJ often finds himself questioning his actions and behavior, wondering if he's good enough or if he's just a pawn in a game where the rules are made by others.

But fret not! There are strategies to combat these negative societal perceptions. One effective approach is to challenge the validity of these judgments. Ask yourself, "Are these criticisms based on facts or mere assumptions?" Often, societal judgments are rooted in stereotypes and misconceptions. By recognizing this, RJ can start to see that these opinions say more about the people who hold them than they do about him. Another strategy is to surround oneself with positive influences. Engaging with uplifting content, whether it's books, podcasts, or social media accounts, can help counteract the negative noise from society.

Now, let's talk about the role of supportive communities in mitigating stigma. Have you ever been part of a group where everyone just gets you? Well, that's what RJ experiences when he's among friends who understand and accept him unconditionally. Supportive communities act as a buffer against the harshness of societal judgment. They provide a safe space where RJ can express himself without fear of ridicule. Being part of such a community can significantly boost his self-esteem and mental well-being. It's like having a shield that deflects the arrows of negativity thrown by society.

Communities can also offer practical assistance. For instance, joining a support group where people share their experiences and coping mechanisms can be incredibly empowering. In these groups, individuals can learn from each other's successes and failures. Moreover, these communities can advocate for change, challenging the societal norms that perpetuate stigma. When RJ sees that others are fighting the same battle, it fosters a sense of solidarity and strength.

Building resilience against external judgment is another key aspect. Think of resilience as a muscle that needs regular exercise to grow stronger. One technique to build this muscle is practicing selfcompassion. Instead of berating himself for perceived flaws, RJ can learn to treat himself with the same kindness and understanding he would offer a friend. Self-compassion can cushion the blow of external criticism. Another technique is cognitive restructuring, which involves identifying and challenging negative thought patterns. For example, instead of thinking, "They must think I'm a failure," RJ could reframe it to, "Their opinion doesn't define my worth."

Additionally, developing a strong sense of identity can help RJ weather the storm of judgment. When he knows who he is and embraces his unique qualities, external opinions lose their power. This confidence can come from reflecting on personal achievements, strengths, and values. It's like having an internal compass that keeps him grounded, regardless of the turbulent winds outside.

Mindfulness practices can also bolster resilience. Techniques such as meditation and deep breathing can help RJ stay centered and present, reducing the impact of external negativity. These practices encourage a focus on the here and now, rather than getting lost in the labyrinth of societal expectations. They train the mind to observe thoughts and judgments without getting entangled in them.

Overthinking: When RJ's self-talk becomes excessive

Let's face it: RJ's brain has a tendency to race faster than a caffeinated hamster on a wheel. Overthinking isn't just a quirk; it's a habit that can wreak havoc on his mental well-being. It's like having an annoying roommate who won't stop talking about Bitcoin, especially when you're trying to sleep or focus on something important.

First things first, let's get into the nitty-gritty of what triggers RJ's overthinking. Picture this: RJ is about to give a presentation at work. He starts to doubt whether he remembered all the key points and worries if his colleagues will judge him harshly for any mistakes. This anxiety builds up even before he steps up to the podium. Triggers often include high-pressure situations, fear of judgment, and past experiences where things didn't go as planned. By recognizing these triggers, RJ can start managing them more effectively. After all, you wouldn't walk through a minefield without knowing where the mines are, right?

Now, let's see how overthinking magnifies stress and anxiety. Imagine RJ sitting at his desk, replaying every single word he said during a meeting. Did he offend someone? Did he sound stupid? Before he knows it, his mind spirals out of control, turning minor concerns into catastrophic failures. Overthinking creates a loop of negative thoughts that amplifies stress and anxiety. It's like turning the volume up on a bad song—you just want it to stop, but it keeps getting louder.

Stress and anxiety are not just abstract feelings; they have physical consequences too. RJ might find himself dealing with headaches, muscle tension, or even digestive issues because of constant overthinking. It's like carrying an invisible backpack filled with rocks, making every step feel heavier and more exhausting. The connection between mind and body here is undeniable, and it's crucial to address both facets to improve overall well-being.

So, what can RJ do to break this cycle of excessive rumination? One effective method is to set time limits for worrying. Let's say RJ allocates 15 minutes a day for his "worry time." During this period, he can jot down all his concerns and get them out of his system. Once the timer goes off, he moves on to something else, preferably something enjoyable. This practice helps in compartmentalizing worries rather than letting them spill over into every part of his day.

Another strategy is to challenge the irrational thoughts. For instance, if RJ fears he'll mess up his presentation, he should ask himself, "What's the worst that could happen?" Often, the feared outcomes are exaggerated and unlikely. By examining these thoughts critically, he can deflate their power over his mind. Sometimes writing them down and evaluating their validity can be eye-opening and liberating.

Distraction techniques also come in handy. Engaging in activities like exercise, hobbies, or spending time with friends can take RJ's mind off the endless loop of overthinking. Think of these distractions as hitting the pause button on a chaotic playlist. They provide a much-needed break and allow space for positive experiences to seep in.

Mindfulness practices are another game-changer. Simple exercises such as deep breathing, meditation, or even mindful walking can center RJ and bring his attention back to the present moment. When RJ notices his mind wandering into overthinking territory, he can gently guide it back to the here and now. This practice not only reduces overthinking but also promotes a sense of calm and groundedness.

An example of a mindfulness exercise is the 5-4-3-2-1 technique. RJ can use this method to ground himself by identifying five things he can see, four things he can touch, three things he can hear, two things he can smell, and one thing he can taste. This sensory exercise can snap him out of a whirlwind of thoughts and anchor him firmly in the present.

Journaling can also be incredibly beneficial. By writing down his thoughts and feelings, RJ gains a clearer perspective on what's bothering him. The act of putting pen to paper can be cathartic, helping to release pent-up emotions and reduce mental clutter. Plus, looking back at journal entries can provide insights into recurring patterns and triggers, offering additional clues on how to tackle them.

The ultimate goal here is to transform RJ's internal dialogue from a relentless critic to a supportive coach. Instead of tearing himself down, RJ needs to learn to build himself up. Positive affirmations and self-compassion are essential components of this transformation. When RJ starts to overthink, he can remind himself of his strengths and achievements. It's like having a motivational poster in your head, cheering you on.

Incorporating humor can also lighten the mental load. Laughter truly is the best medicine, and finding the funny side of a stressful situation can make it more manageable. By taking himself—and his thoughts—a little less seriously, RJ can alleviate some of the pressure he puts on himself. After all, life's too short to spend it in a never-ending cycle of worry.

Negative Self-Talk: The danger of internal criticism for RJ

Negative self-talk is like an inner gremlin that lurks in the shadows of RJ's mind, waiting to pounce on any opportunity to sow doubt and fear. Recognizing patterns of self-criticism is the first step in taming this pesky gremlin. Have you ever caught yourself thinking, "I'm such an idiot" after making a simple mistake? Or perhaps you've berated yourself with thoughts like, "I'll never be good enough"? These are classic examples of self-critical patterns. It's as if we all have an inner critic armed with a megaphone, ready to amplify our insecurities.

These harmful thought loops often seem harmless at first glance, but they slowly chip away at RJ's confidence. Picture RJ standing at the edge of a diving board, ready to leap into the pool, only to be held back by the incessant voice saying, "What if everyone laughs at you?" This kind of internal dialogue can paralyze action and inhibit personal growth. The impact of negative self-talk extends beyond individual moments and trickles into various aspects of life, including personal achievements and relationships.

When RJ's internal critic has free rein, it can diminish the sense of accomplishment even before he gets started. Imagine RJ working tirelessly on a project, only to think, "This isn't good enough; someone else could do it better." Such thoughts prevent RJ from celebrating his efforts and successes. Over time, this can lead to a lack of motivation. As for relationships, negative self-talk can create barriers that prevent genuine connections. If RJ believes he's not worthy of love or friendship, he may withdraw from social interactions, further isolating himself and reinforcing the negative narrative.

But fear not, there is light at the end of this tunnel! Cognitive restructuring techniques provide a beacon of hope for challenging these detrimental thoughts. Consider cognitive restructuring as giving RJ's inner gremlin a much-needed makeover. Instead of letting that gremlin shout, "You're a failure," RJ can train himself to respond with,

"I'm learning and growing from my experiences." This technique involves identifying negative thoughts, evaluating their validity, and replacing them with more balanced and realistic perspectives.

For example, let's say RJ catches himself thinking, "No one likes me." With cognitive restructuring, he would examine the evidence for and against this thought. Perhaps he recalls instances where friends reached out to him or moments when colleagues praised his work. By focusing on these positive events, RJ can counteract the negative thought with a more accurate statement: "I have people in my life who appreciate me."

Building a positive inner dialogue is another crucial step in transforming RJ's mental landscape. It's like planting a garden; you need to nurture it regularly for it to flourish. Instead of allowing weeds of negativity to take root, RJ can plant seeds of positivity through affirmations and self-compassion. Affirmations are positive statements that reinforce confidence and resilience. For instance, RJ might start each day with, "I am capable, and I deserve good things." Repeating these affirmations helps to create new neural pathways, gradually overshadowing the old, negative ones.

Self-compassion also plays a vital role in cultivating a healthier inner dialogue. Often, we are kinder to others than we are to ourselves. Encouraging RJ to treat himself with the same kindness and understanding he would offer a friend can be a game-changer. When RJ makes a mistake, rather than scolding himself harshly, he can practice self-compassion by acknowledging his humanity and offering gentle reassurance. A phrase like, "It's okay to make mistakes; it's part of being human," can go a long way in fostering a supportive internal environment.

Developing self-compassion can also involve mindfulness practices. By staying present and observing his thoughts without judgment, RJ can create space between himself and his inner critic. Mindfulness allows RJ to recognize when negative self-talk arises and choose a compassionate response instead of reacting automatically. Techniques such as deep breathing, meditation, or even journaling about his thoughts and feelings can help RJ stay grounded and maintain a positive outlook.

An additional strategy RJ can use is visualizing success and practicing gratitude. Visualization exercises involve imagining himself succeeding in various scenarios, which can boost his confidence and prepare him mentally for real-life challenges. Gratitude practices, such as keeping a daily gratitude journal, help shift focus from what's lacking to appreciating what he already has. This shift in perspective can significantly enhance RJ's overall wellbeing and promote a positive inner dialogue.

Creating a community of support is also beneficial in maintaining a positive inner dialogue. Surrounding himself with encouraging and uplifting individuals can reinforce RJ's efforts to silence his inner critic. Feedback from trusted friends or mentors can provide valuable perspectives, helping RJ see himself in a more positive light. Additionally, engaging in supportive group activities or seeking professional help, such as therapy or counseling, can provide RJ with the tools and support he needs to continue building on these newfound skills.

Distraction: RJ losing focus due to constant internal chatter

Ah, internal distractions—the sneaky little gremlins that sabotage productivity just when you think you're on a roll. For RJ, these internal distractions are more than just momentary lapses in focus; they can be persistent hurdles to achieving both daily tasks and long-term goals.

First off, let's dive into how we identify these pesky intruders. Internal distractions often stem from various sources such as worries about the future, regrets from the past, or even mundane thoughts like what's for dinner. RJ frequently finds himself caught in these thought spirals. Sometimes it's work-related concerns—an upcoming project deadline, for instance—other times, it could be personal anxieties over relationships or finances. Recognizing these sources is the first step in tackling them. RJ has started keeping a journal, jotting down whenever he notices his mind wandering. This practice not only helps him identify patterns but also serves as a reality check; sometimes seeing your scattered thoughts on paper makes them seem less daunting.

Once you've identified these distractions, it's important to understand their influence. Mental noise can drastically impact RJ's ability to perform daily tasks efficiently and stay committed to his long-term objectives. Imagine RJ is working on an important report but keeps ruminating over something trivial, like the awkward conversation he had with a colleague last week. This distraction can lead to mistakes, decreased output, and eventually, procrastination. Over time, these small diversions accumulate, causing significant setbacks in achieving larger goals. It's like trying to drive with the parking brake on—you'll get somewhere, but it'll take twice as much effort and time.

So, how can RJ improve concentration and mental clarity? One effective technique is mindfulness meditation, which involves focusing on the present moment and gently steering away from distracting thoughts. RJ finds that setting aside just ten minutes each morning for mindfulness exercises significantly improves his focus throughout the day. Another useful tool is the Pomodoro Technique, where RJ works for 25-minute intervals followed by a short break. This method creates a balanced workflow that keeps distractions at bay while maintaining high levels of productivity.

Next up, practices for maintaining focus amidst disruptive thoughts. Realistically, it's impossible to eliminate all internal distractions, but RJ can certainly learn to manage them. A quick go-to method for RJ is deep breathing exercises, especially when he's feeling particularly overwhelmed. By taking slow, deep breaths, he calms his nervous system and refocuses his mind. Another powerful practice involves setting clear, specific goals for each day. Instead of having a vague idea of what needs to get done, RJ writes down precise tasks. This structure gives him a roadmap to follow and minimizes the space for wandering thoughts.

Physical activity also plays a crucial role in maintaining focus. When RJ incorporates regular exercise into his routine, he notices a significant improvement in his ability to concentrate. Exercise releases endorphins, which help reduce stress and improve mood, making it easier to stay focused on tasks at hand. Even something as simple as a brisk walk during lunch breaks can refresh the mind and boost productivity.

Of course, technology can both be a friend and a foe when it comes to managing internal dialogue. While notifications and social media can easily become sources of distraction, RJ leverages productivity apps designed to keep him on track. Tools like Focus@Will provide ambient music tailored to enhance concentration, while apps like Forest gamify staying focused by growing virtual trees as long as you avoid using your phone.

Another strategy RJ uses is the "Two-Minute Rule," inspired by productivity expert David Allen. If a task takes two minutes or less to complete, RJ does it immediately rather than letting it clutter his mind and to-do list. This approach reduces the cognitive load, allowing him to focus better on more significant tasks without the constant nagging of small, unfinished chores.

RJ also experiments with visual reminders. Sticky notes with motivational quotes or essential tasks placed around his workspace act as gentle nudges to stay on course. Seeing a note that says, "Focus on one thing at a time," can be remarkably grounding when his mind starts drifting.

Social support shouldn't be underestimated either. RJ realizes that discussing his struggles with trusted friends or colleagues can provide new perspectives and solutions he hadn't considered. Just talking through his internal distractions often brings relief and renewed focus.

It's also important to create a conducive physical environment. RJ ensures his workspace is tidy and free from unnecessary clutter. A clean, organized desk can work wonders for mental clarity. Additionally, proper lighting and a comfortable chair contribute to maintaining focus without physical discomfort becoming another distraction.

Hydration and nutrition also play subtle yet vital roles. RJ keeps a water bottle within reach and chooses brain-boosting snacks like nuts or fruits over sugary treats that lead to energy crashes. Maintaining a balanced diet supports overall cognitive function, which in turn aids concentration.

Lastly, RJ practices self-compassion. Understanding that it's okay to have moments of distraction allows him to reset without harsh selfcriticism. A kind inner dialogue encourages perseverance and resilience, making it easier to regain focus after a lapse.

The Volume Control Conundrum: When RJ's Inner Voice Gets Loud

As RJ became more comfortable with his self-talk, he encountered a new challenge: volume control. It seemed his inner voice hadn't quite grasped the concept of an "inside voice," leading to some rather awkward situations.

One peaceful Saturday morning, RJ was engrossed in a particularly tricky coding problem. As he often did, he began talking through the issue out loud:

"Okay, so if we implement the algorithm here, it should reduce the processing time. But wait, what about memory usage? Hmm, tradeoffs, trade-offs..."

Lost in thought, RJ's voice gradually increased in volume until he was practically shouting:

"AHA! If we use a hash table instead, we can optimize both time AND space complexity!"

It wasn't until he heard a timid knock on his apartment wall that RJ realized just how loud he'd become. His neighbor's muffled voice came through:

"Um, RJ? I'm glad you solved your... hash table crisis? But some of us are trying to sleep..."

Red-faced, RJ called back an apology, making a mental note to work on his volume control. However, this was easier said than done.

The following week, during a quiet moment in a team meeting, RJ was lost in thought about the project timeline. Without realizing it, he began muttering under his breath:

"If we move the deadline to next month, we'd have more time for testing. But then again, the client might not be happy. Decisions, decisions..."

It wasn't until he noticed the entire room had gone silent, all eyes on him, that RJ realized he'd been thinking "out loud" again. His colleagues stared at him, a mix of confusion and amusement on their faces.

"Oh, don't mind me," RJ said with a nervous laugh. "I'm just... practicing my ventriloquism. You know, in case this coding thing doesn't work out."

From that day on, RJ's coworkers started jokingly referring to his mutterings as "RJ Radio" – tune in for coding tips, random musings, and the occasional impromptu debate.

Another unexpected pitfall arose when RJ decided to brush up on his foreign language skills. He had always heard that talking to yourself in another language was a great way to practice, but he didn't anticipate the confusion it would cause.

RJ began by practicing Spanish, holding conversations with himself while doing chores:

"¿Dónde está la biblioteca?" he asked his reflection in the mirror while brushing his teeth. "La biblioteca está... uh... en mi corazón?"

As he grew more confident, RJ started mixing languages, creating a sort of linguistic smoothie in his head. This led to some interesting moments, like when he was ordering coffee one morning:

"Puedo... ich möchte... um... one café, s'il vous plaît?" he stammered to the bewildered barista.

The poor barista, unsure which language to respond in, simply held up a coffee cup with a questioning look. RJ nodded enthusiastically, relieved that caffeine was a universal language recognised across the Galaxy.

His multilingual self-talk reached new heights of confusion during a team brainstorming session. As ideas were being thrown around, RJ's inner voice chimed in:

"Zhu yi! Das ist eine ausgezeichnete idée! We should implement it pronto!"

It wasn't until he saw his colleagues' baffled expressions that RJ realized he'd said it out loud, in a baffling mix of Chinese, German, French, and English.

"Sorry," he said sheepishly. "Sometimes my inner voice likes to show off its Duolingo achievements."

The Imaginary Audience Syndrome: RJ's Inner TED Talk

As RJ's self-talk habit evolved, he developed a tendency to turn his inner monologues into full-blown presentations, complete with an imaginary audience. This "Imaginary Audience Syndrome" led to some entertaining scenarios.

While cooking dinner one evening, RJ found himself delivering a passionate speech about the importance of proper pasta-to-sauce ratios:

"Ladies and gentlemen," he announced to his kitchen utensils, "today we stand on the precipice of a culinary revolution. No longer shall we be slaves to arbitrary sauce measurements!"

He was so engrossed in his presentation, gesticulating with a saucecovered spoon, that he didn't notice his roommate had entered the kitchen. It wasn't until he heard a slow clap that RJ turned around, sauce dripping down his arm, to see his roommate giving him a standing ovation.

"Bravo!" his roommate cheered. "Does this mean you're finally going to stop drowning your spaghetti in sauce?"

RJ's tendency to turn everything into a TED talk didn't stop at home. During a routine dental check-up, he began explaining the intricacies of flossing techniques to his imaginary audience:

"Now, you might think the simple back-and-forth motion is enough," he mumbled around the dentist's fingers, "but let me introduce you to the revolutionary concept of the floss tango!"

The dentist, used to patients making odd noises, simply nodded along, though she did make a note to recommend a stress ball for her enthusiastic patient.

The Constant Narrator: RJ 's Life as a David Attenborough Documentary

Perhaps one of the most persistent pitfalls RJ encountered was his brain's newfound love for narrating his life as if it were a nature documentary. It was as if David Attenborough had taken up permanent residence in his head.

During a particularly uneventful day at the office, RJ found his inner voice providing commentary:

"Here we see the wild programmer in his natural habitat," the voice intoned as RJ scrolled through pages of code. "Watch as he navigates the treacherous waters of legacy code, skillfully avoiding the sharp reefs of outdated functions."

This constant narration, while entertaining, sometimes made it hard for RJ to focus on actual work. It reached a peak during a company fire drill:

"And now, the herd begins its biannual migration," RJ muttered as he joined his colleagues filing out of the building. "Notice how they move in a unified, yet chaotic pattern, drawn by the siren song of potential danger and the promise of a break from spreadsheets."

It wasn't until his manager shot him a quizzical look that RJ realized he'd been narrating out loud. "Just... providing some color commentary," he explained weakly. "You know, to make fire drills more exciting."

From that day on, RJ's coworkers started jokingly calling him "The Narrator," often asking him to provide commentary for mundane office events. Little did they know, they were only hearing a fraction of the constant documentary playing in RJ's head.

As RJ navigated these new pitfalls, he couldn't help but laugh at the absurdity of it all. Sure, his self-talk habit had its challenges, but it also made life infinitely more interesting. After all, who else could say they had an internal radio station, a multilingual debate club, a TED talk series, and a nature documentary all playing in their head at once?

"Well, RJ," he said to himself as he settled in for bed one night, "life with you is certainly never boring. Here's to more adventures in the wild world of self-talk – just maybe with a little less volume and a lot less public narration."

And with that, RJ drifted off to sleep, his dreams a wild mix of coding problems, pasta-based revolutions, and a documentary about the sleeping habits of computer programmers, all narrated in a medley of languages. Just another day in the life of RJ, the selftalking extraordinaire.

Final Thoughts

RJ's journey through internal dialogue takes us from the nagging whispers of social stigma to the endless loops of overthinking and the relentless grip of negative self-talk. By recognizing how external voices shape our self-perception, RJ learns to challenge unfair judgments and surround himself with positive influences. Supportive communities become his sanctuary, offering both emotional refuge and practical strategies to combat societal negativity. Just like practicing self-compassion and mindfulness to build resilience, RJ realizes that transforming inner dialogue into a supportive coach involves consistent effort and kindness.

As RJ confronts the noisy gremlins of distraction, he develops techniques to stay focused amidst chaos. Mindfulness exercises, structured goal setting, and even simple tools like sticky notes and productivity apps become his allies. Regular exercise and a balanced diet enhance his mental clarity, while a tidy workspace creates an environment conducive to concentration. Through these steps, RJ not only manages his internal chatter but also turns it into a source of strength. Remember, tackling these internal hurdles isn't about perfection; it's about progress and creating a kinder, more focused inner world.

Part IV: The Science

Exploring Self-Talk: A Multidisciplinary Approach

Exploring self-talk is like discovering a secret superpower you never knew you had. Imagine having a 24/7 personal coach, therapist, and brainstorming buddy all rolled into one, ready to help you navigate life's ups and downs. Whether you're planning your day, calming your nerves before a big meeting, or evaluating the pros and cons of a decision, that little voice inside your head is always there to lend a hand. Part IV dives deep into understanding how this constant inner chatter shapes our thoughts, emotions, and actions.

But we're not just scratching the surface here; we're taking a full-on multidisciplinary plunge. Prepare yourself for a safari through the jungles of cognitive psychology, where you'll see how inner speech functions as a tool for problem-solving. Get ready to light up your neural pathways with insights from neuroscience, explaining what happens in your brain during self-talk. Then, pack your cultural suitcase as we journey around the world to discover how different societies view talking to oneself. Finally, we'll take a stroll down history lane, meeting famous figures who mastered the art of selftalk to achieve greatness. Buckle up—this is going to be an enlightening and entertaining ride!

Little did RJ know, he was about to embark on a wild ride through the landscape of cognitive psychology, neuroscience, and cultural perspectives. Buckle up, folks – we're about to take a trip through RJ's brain on science!

Cognitive Psychology: Understanding the Role of Inner Speech

RJ's first stop on his scientific journey was cognitive psychology. He imagined himself as an intrepid explorer, hacking through the dense jungle of psychological theories with a machete made of curiosity (and perhaps a bit too much caffeine).

As he delved into the research, RJ learned that inner speech, or verbal thinking, plays a crucial role in cognitive functions like problem-solving, self-regulation, and memory. It was as if his brain had been secretly training for a cognitive Olympics all this time!

"So you're telling me," RJ mused to himself, "that all those times I was talking to myself about code, I was actually enhancing my problem-solving skills? Ha! Take that, judgmental coworkers!"

He even found studies suggesting that inner speech helps with task switching and planning. RJ couldn't help but feel a sense of vindication:

"You see? When I'm having a full-blown conversation with myself about whether to tackle bug fixes or start a new feature, I'm not procrastinating – I'm optimizing my cognitive resources!"

But the real game-changer came when RJ stumbled upon research about the role of self-talk in emotional regulation. Scientists had found that positive self-talk could help manage stress and boost confidence.

"Well, well, well," RJ grinned, "looks like all those pep talks I've been giving myself aren't just hot air. They're scientifically-backed hot air!"

Armed with this knowledge, RJ decided to put it to the test. The next time he faced a challenging coding problem, instead of his usual frustrated grumbling, he tried a more positive approach:

"Alright, RJ, you've got this. You're the Sherlock Holmes of debugging. This code doesn't stand a chance against your intellectual magnifying glass!"

To his surprise (and his neighboring cubicle's relief), RJ found himself feeling more confident and less stressed. He even solved the problem faster than usual.

"Elementary, my dear me," he chuckled, tipping an imaginary deerstalker hat to his reflection in the computer screen.Inner speech, that little voice inside our heads, isn't just there for the fun of it. It functions as a highly practical tool for thinking and problemsolving. Imagine trying to solve an algebra problem or plan a route for your weekend errands without talking yourself through it. Inner speech allows us to process information internally, creating a mental workspace where ideas can be manipulated and refined until we land on a solution.

Consider this: when faced with a dilemma, you often run through different scenarios in your mind, weighing pros and cons. This internal dialogue helps you make more informed decisions by allowing you to evaluate options and their potential consequences. It's like having a brainstorming session with yourself. Inner speech helps filter out less viable solutions and zeroes in on the best course of action.

Now, let's talk about emotions and behaviors. Oh yes, inner speech has something to say here too—quite literally! When you're upset or anxious, your internal dialogue can help regulate your emotions. Think of those moments when you've told yourself to calm down or reassured yourself that everything will be fine. Inner speech provides a mental space for self-regulation, which is crucial for maintaining emotional balance. It's like having your own personal therapist available 24/7, helping you navigate life's emotional roller coasters.

But wait, there's more! Inner speech also plays a prominent role in working memory. You know, that cognitive scratchpad we use to hold and manipulate information temporarily. When you're trying to remember a phone number or follow complex instructions, inner speech helps keep that information in your mind's eye. By repeating things over and over in your head, you're essentially using inner speech to bolster your memory and improve cognitive performance.

And who doesn't love a bit of introspection now and then? Inner speech is a key player when it comes to self-reflection and personal development. It's through this quiet dialogue with ourselves that we make sense of our experiences and develop personal narratives. These narratives shape our identities and influence how we interact with the world. Whether it's reflecting on past mistakes or dreaming about future aspirations, inner speech provides the canvas for these thoughts to unfold.

Let's break this down with an example. Imagine Jane, an aspiring author, uses her inner speech to draft and refine her story ideas before putting pen to paper. She debates plot twists, character arcs, and thematic elements internally, ironing out details long before they hit the page. In essence, her inner speech acts as a sounding board, enabling her to enhance her creative output.

In another instance, consider Joe, who has recently started a new job and feels overwhelmed by the responsibilities. By engaging in inner speech, he talks himself through the tasks, reassuring himself of his abilities and formulating strategies to tackle challenges. Over time, this self-talk becomes a potent tool for boosting his confidence and enhancing his performance at work.

Furthermore, inner speech isn't just about serious stuff; it can add some humor into the mix. When we catch ourselves making silly mistakes, that mental chuckle or light-hearted self-commentary can diffuse tension and bring a smile to our faces. It's like having an internal comic relief act on standby—a gentle reminder not to take life too seriously.

Let's not forget that inner speech can also aid in managing stress. Picture this: Lisa is preparing for an important presentation. Naturally, she's nervous. However, by engaging in positive self-talk, she bolsters her confidence, reminding herself of her preparation and capabilities. This mental pep talk can significantly reduce her anxiety, paving the way for a successful presentation.

Interestingly, inner speech evolves with us. Children often engage in external self-talk, vocalizing their thoughts as they navigate the world around them. As they grow older, this external dialogue gradually transforms into silent inner speech. This transition marks a significant milestone in cognitive development, highlighting the importance of inner speech in shaping thought processes and behavior.

Moreover, inner speech offers a unique platform for rehearsing and practicing social interactions. Before a big date or an important meeting, many people run through potential conversations in their minds, considering different responses and outcomes. This mental rehearsal not only boosts confidence but also prepares individuals for real-life interactions, enhancing their social skills.

Neuroscience: What Happens in the Brain During Self-Talk

Emboldened by his foray into cognitive psychology, RJ decided to go deeper – quite literally – into the brain. Neuroscience, he discovered, was like the CSI of the mind, revealing the behind-the-scenes action of his chatty neurons.

RJ learned that during self-talk, various regions of the brain light up like a Christmas tree. The left inferior frontal gyrus, involved in speech production, gets particularly active.

"So, when I'm talking to myself," RJ mused, "my brain is essentially hosting its own little rave. Explains why I sometimes get a headache after particularly intense internal debates."

He was fascinated to discover that self-talk activates many of the same brain regions as external speech. It was as if his brain couldn't tell the difference between RJ talking to himself and RJ talking to, well, anyone else.

"No wonder my brain keeps falling for its own jokes," RJ chuckled. "It thinks I'm a stand-up comedian performing for a live audience!"

But the real mind-blower came when RJ learned about the default mode network (DMN) – a set of brain regions active when we're not focused on the outside world. This network plays a role in selfreflection and daydreaming.

"Hold on," RJ gasped, nearly spilling his coffee, "you're telling me there's a whole network in my brain dedicated to zoning out and talking to myself? It's like I've got a built-in comedy club up there!"

Excited by this discovery, RJ couldn't resist sharing it with his colleagues. During the next team meeting, as the discussion droned on about quarterly reports, RJ found his mind wandering. Suddenly, he blurted out:

"Did you know we have a default mode network that's active when we're not paying attention to stuff like... uh... quarterly reports?"

The room fell silent. His manager raised an eyebrow.

"I mean," RJ backpedaled, "not that I'm not paying attention. My default mode network is totally offline right now. Fully engaged. Quarterly reports. Yay."

From that day on, whenever RJ seemed distracted, his colleagues would jokingly ask if his "default mode network" was acting up again.

Understanding the neurological basis of self-talk can seem like diving headfirst into a bustling city – there's always something happening, and every corner turned reveals another complex interaction. At the heart of all this activity is the prefrontal cortex, which plays a vital role in generating and regulating our inner dialogue. This region of the brain is like the city's central command center, overseeing executive functions such as planning, decisionmaking, and, you guessed it, self-talk. Imagine the prefrontal cortex as a meticulous planner at an event; it's constantly juggling tasks, ensuring everything runs smoothly and according to plan.

But the prefrontal cortex doesn't work alone. It recruits other areas of the brain to engage in self-talk, akin to delegating tasks to trusted team members. Neural imaging studies have shown that language areas like Broca's area and Wernicke's area light up during inner speech. Think of these regions as the chatty townsfolk who love to gossip – they are deeply involved in the construction and comprehension of language, whether spoken out loud or kept within the confines of one's mind. Essentially, when we talk to ourselves, we're utilizing much of the same neural machinery that we do for conversations with others. So next time someone catches you muttering to yourself, you can confidently claim you're just keeping your neural networks well-oiled!

Now, while our prefrontal cortex and language areas are doing the heavy lifting, the type of self-talk we engage in can shift the entire dynamic of our neural city. Different patterns of brain activity emerge depending on whether our inner dialogue is positive or negative. Positive self-talk is like having a cheerleader in your brain, boosting motivation, confidence, and overall morale. On the flip side, negative self-talk acts more like a strict drill sergeant, often activating stress responses and sapping energy. Research has shown that these different tones of self-talk produce distinct neural pathways. For example, positive self-talk tends to engage rewardprocessing regions, promoting feelings of joy and satisfaction. In contrast, negative self-talk can activate areas associated with stress and anxiety, painting a much gloomier picture.

Adding yet another layer to this intricate web are neurotransmitters like dopamine and serotonin, the brain's very own chemical messengers. Like diligent postal workers, they deliver messages that influence our mood and motivation, thereby affecting how we talk to ourselves. Dopamine, often dubbed the 'feel-good' neurotransmitter, plays a critical role in reward and pleasure systems. When levels of dopamine are high, our inner dialogue is likely to be more upbeat and encouraging. On the other hand, lower levels can result in selftalk that feels more like a scolding.

Serotonin also steps onto the stage, bringing its own set of influences. Often associated with mood regulation, serotonin impacts how we perceive and react to situations. Higher levels generally promote a sense of well-being and stability, fostering kinder self-talk. Conversely, low levels of serotonin can lead to negative, self-critical inner dialogue. It's like having two distinct radio stations in your brain: one playing upbeat tunes that keep you motivated, and the other spinning melancholic tracks that bring you down.

To put it all together, think of the brain as a fantastical banquet where each guest has their unique role to play. The prefrontal cortex is the host, orchestrating the event and managing logistics. Broca's area and Wernicke's area are the eloquent speakers, engaging in lively discussion. Meanwhile, the emotional tone of the gathering is set by the interplay of positive and negative vibes, influenced by our neurotransmitters. It's a never-ending party where everyone contributes to the ongoing conversation of self-talk.

This complex interaction of brain regions and chemicals underscores the profound impact of self-talk on our lives. Understanding the neurological basis of self-talk not only demystifies the experience but also empowers us to influence our inner dialogue consciously. By nurturing positive self-talk, we can create a healthier mental environment, much like ensuring that the city's infrastructure is robust and resilient. So, next time you catch yourself in a loop of negative thinking, remember that you're the city's mayor, capable of implementing policies that encourage a more supportive and uplifting internal narrative.

Cultural Perspectives: How Different Societies View Talking to Oneself

In exploring cultural variations in attitudes toward self-talk, we embark on a fascinating journey through different societies and their unique perspectives. Self-talk, the act of speaking to oneself either out loud or silently, can be found across all cultures. However, the interpretation and acceptability of self-talk vary greatly, shaped by historical, spiritual, and societal influences.

Let's begin with Eastern cultures. In many Eastern traditions, selftalk is often intertwined with practices of meditation and mindfulness. Rather than being seen as a mere cognitive exercise, it becomes an essential part of a holistic approach to life. Picture a serene monk sitting cross-legged, eyes closed, uttering silent affirmations. Here, self-talk is a tool for achieving mental clarity and self-awareness. This practice helps individuals focus their minds and remain present in the moment. Mindfulness practices such as these are believed to reduce stress, improve concentration, and foster a deeper connection with one's true self. In countries like Japan, China, and India, this form of self-reflection is encouraged as a way to harmonize the mind, body, and spirit.

Switching gears to Western societies, self-talk is predominantly viewed through a psychological lens. The phrase "talk to yourself" often conjures images of motivational speakers urging us to embrace positive self-talk for self-improvement. In this context, self-talk is not just idle chatter but a powerful mechanism for cognitive restructuring. Imagine someone preparing for a big presentation, repeating phrases like, "I can do this," or "I am confident." Psychologists have long recognized self-talk as a vital component of cognitive-behavioral therapy (CBT). By identifying and challenging negative thoughts, individuals can reframe their inner dialogue to promote a more positive and constructive mindset. It's all about boosting one's confidence, enhancing performance, and fostering resilience in the face of adversity. In Western culture, the mantra is clear: if you want to change your life, start by changing your inner conversation.

Now, let's venture into indigenous cultures, where the concept of self-talk takes on a profoundly spiritual dimension. For many indigenous communities, self-talk is not merely a conversation with oneself but a dialogue with spiritual entities or ancestors. Consider a Native American elder engaging in a monologue that seems directed at the heavens. Here, speaking to oneself is deeply embedded in broader spiritual practices. It's a way to seek guidance, wisdom, and comfort from those who have passed on, blurring the lines between the physical and the spiritual realms. This form of self-talk often involves rituals, chants, or meditative states, underscoring its significance as a sacred communication channel. The practice reinforces communal values, links the present with the ancestral past, and infuses everyday life with spiritual meaning.

The acceptability and interpretation of self-talk can differ dramatically based on societal norms and values. In some places, talking to oneself might be viewed with suspicion or concern. Imagine strolling down a busy street while having an animated conversation with yourself. In certain contexts, this behavior could be misinterpreted as a sign of madness or instability. Historically, individuals exhibiting such behavior were often stigmatized or ostracized. Even today, misconceptions about self-talk persist, sometimes resulting in undue stigma or misunderstanding.

On the other hand, many contemporary societies increasingly recognize self-talk as a legitimate tool for personal growth and mental well-being. Take, for example, the world of sports, where athletes frequently use self-talk strategies to enhance performance.

A basketball player might silently recite, "Focus on the shot," before making a crucial free throw. This technique, known as performanceenhancing self-talk, has been widely studied and validated within sports psychology. It's all about harnessing the power of internal dialogue to overcome challenges, maintain composure, and achieve peak performance.

Furthermore, the manner in which self-talk is perceived can evolve over time. Cultural evolution plays a significant role in shaping our attitudes towards self-talk. For instance, what was once considered taboo or eccentric may gradually gain acceptance as scientific understanding and societal attitudes progress. Today, the emphasis on mental health and well-being has brought self-talk into the mainstream, highlighting its potential benefits for anyone willing to engage in a little introspection.

Ultimately, the diversity in attitudes toward self-talk highlights the intricate relationship between culture and individual behavior. Whether it serves as a meditative practice, a psychological tool, a spiritual dialogue, or a method for personal growth, self-talk remains a universal phenomenon influenced by the values, beliefs, and traditions of each society. By appreciating these cultural variations, we gain a richer understanding of self-talk's multifaceted nature and its profound impact on human experience.

Historical Figures: Famous Self-Talkers Throughout History

As RJ delved deeper into his research, he was thrilled to discover that he was in good company when it came to talking to oneself.

History was filled with famous self-talkers!

"You're telling me," RJ exclaimed to his laptop, "that some of the greatest minds in history were chatting away to themselves too? I'm practically royalty!"

He learned about Charles Dickens, who would act out his characters in front of a mirror, having animated conversations with himself.

"Note to self," RJ muttered, "invest in a bigger mirror. If it worked for Dickens, it could work for debugging code!"

Then there was Nikola Tesla, known for memorizing entire books and having discussions about them with imaginary friends.

"Imaginary friends, eh?" RJ mused. "I wonder if Siri counts. She's been privy to some pretty intense debates about the merits of different programming languages."

But the historical figure that really caught RJ's attention was Albert Einstein. The famous physicist was known to talk to himself softly, repeating certain words and phrases.

This discovery led to a new phase in RJ's self-talk journey. He began prefacing his coding sessions with a ritual:

"I am Einstein. E equals MC squared. Relativity is relative to relatively relative relatives... Okay, I have no idea what I'm saying, but I feel smarter already!"

His colleagues were puzzled by his new habit of muttering physics equations under his breath, but they had to admit – his code did seem to be getting better.

"It's all relative," RJ would say with a wink whenever anyone asked about his improved performance.

As RJ concluded his scientific exploration of self-talk, he felt a newfound appreciation for his chatty habit. It wasn't just a quirk – it was a cognitive tool, a neurological phenomenon, a cultural experience, and a link to some of history's greatest minds.

"Well, brain," RJ said to himself as he leaned back in his chair, "looks like we're not just talking to ourselves. We're participating in a grand tradition of cognitive science, neurobiology, anthropology, and history. Not bad for a couple of chatty neurons, eh?"

With a grin, RJ turned back to his computer, ready to face his next coding challenge. After all, with science on his side and Einstein in his head, what couldn't he accomplish?

"Let's do this," he declared to himself. "For science! For history! For the love of a good internal monologue!"

And with that, RJ dove back into his work, his inner voice chattering away happily, now backed by the full weight of scientific research. Who knew that talking to oneself could be so intellectually stimulating?Winston Churchill, the stalwart British Prime Minister during World War II, was known for his persuasive speeches and unyielding confidence. But behind his public facade lay a lesserknown secret: self-talk. Churchill often used self-talk as a tool to boost his confidence and rehearse his speeches. In times of doubt or when preparing for pivotal moments, he would engage in inner dialogues, critiquing and refining his oratory skills. This mental rehearsal played a significant role in his ability to deliver impactful and memorable speeches. By using self-talk effectively, Churchill was able to maintain a confident, composed persona that rallied and inspired a nation during its darkest hours.

Nikola Tesla, the visionary inventor responsible for so many modern technological advancements, also utilized self-talk. Tesla frequently engaged in detailed inner dialogues to mentally visualize and test his inventions before ever building them. He had an extraordinary ability to conduct experiments entirely in his mind, running complex simulations and making adjustments through self-directed conversations. This mental process allowed him to foresee potential flaws and perfect his designs without the need for physical prototypes. Tesla's method of using self-talk as a mental laboratory showcases the profound impact of inner dialogue on innovation and creativity. His inventive spirit was, in no small part, fueled by these intricate internal discussions.

Eleanor Roosevelt, one of the most influential First Ladies in American history, faced the challenge of overcoming profound shyness. To build her public persona and become an effective diplomat, she turned to self-talk. Through positive affirmations and internal encouragement, Roosevelt managed to transform her insecurities into strengths. She frequently reminded herself of her capabilities and rehearsed her public appearances mentally, building the confidence required to address large audiences and assert her views on social justice. Roosevelt's use of self-talk enabled her to step out of her comfort zone, becoming a powerful voice for change and cementing her legacy as a champion for human rights.

Renowned psychologist Carl Jung had a distinct approach to selftalk, incorporating it into his broader theoretical framework. Jung explored self-talk through his concept of individuation, which encourages dialogue with different parts of the psyche to achieve personal integration and self-awareness. By speaking with various aspects of oneself—such as the shadow, anima, and animus— individuals could reconcile unconscious conflicts and foster a more harmonious inner life. Jung believed that such internal conversations were essential for achieving wholeness and understanding the complexities of one's personality. Through his studies and practices, Jung demonstrated that self-talk is not just a tool for everyday problem-solving but a profound means of selfdiscovery and psychological growth.

Each of these historical figures demonstrates the versatile applications and benefits of self-talk. Churchill's technique shows its power in boosting confidence and enhancing public speaking skills. Tesla's mental dialogues illustrate how self-talk can drive creative and innovative processes. Roosevelt's experience highlights its role in overcoming personal challenges and building public personas. Finally, Jung's exploration underscores the deep psychological significance of engaging in inner conversations. These examples underscore the effectiveness and multifaceted nature of self-talk, reflecting its vital role across diverse fields and contexts.

Understanding how these notable individuals harnessed self-talk offers valuable lessons for anyone looking to improve their own lives. Emulating Churchill's confidence-boosting techniques can be particularly beneficial for those facing public speaking anxieties or leadership roles. Following Tesla's example, one can use self-talk for creative brainstorming and problem-solving. Roosevelt's practice of positive affirmations can help individuals confront personal insecurities, while Jung's method points to deeper self-reflection and personal growth.

By learning from these historical figures, we can appreciate that selftalk isn't merely about daily affirmations or motivational pep talks. It's a dynamic, multifaceted tool that can aid in overcoming personal challenges, fostering creativity, and achieving personal integration. Whether you're delivering a keynote speech, designing a revolutionary invention, stepping into a new professional role, or delving into the depths of your psyche, self-talk can serve as a powerful companion on your journey.

In essence, self-talk helps bridge the gap between our internal world and external realities. It's a testament to the timeless utility of inner dialogue that such distinguished individuals from varied backgrounds relied on it. Their stories encourage us to explore and utilize self-talk in our own lives, transforming it from a simple habit into a strategic, transformative practice.

As we delve deeper into self-talk's multidisciplinary approaches, these historical lessons provide a foundation. They show us that beneath the surface of great achievements and groundbreaking ideas lies a common thread: the deliberate, thoughtful engagement in conversation with oneself. The next time you find yourself facing a daunting task, remember Churchill's resolute rehearsals, Tesla's intricate mental blueprints, Roosevelt's empowering affirmations, and Jung's insightful explorations. Your inner dialogue might just be the key to unlocking your full potential.

Summary and Reflections

Self-talk is more than just a quirky habit; it's a crucial tool for navigating life's twists and turns. From solving complex problems to managing stress, our inner dialogue plays a key role in shaping our thoughts and actions. We've seen how cognitive psychology highlights the practical uses of self-talk in decision-making and emotional regulation. Neuroscience provides a deeper look at the brain's intricate dance during these internal conversations, shedding light on the powerful influence of neurotransmitters like dopamine and serotonin. Cultural perspectives reveal a rich tapestry of how different societies view talking to oneself, whether as a meditative practice or a motivational technique. And let's not forget the historical figures who harnessed the power of self-talk to achieve great things.

So the next time you catch yourself chatting away inside your head, remember that you're in good company. Whether you're channeling your inner Churchill before a big presentation, tackling a tricky task with Tesla-like creativity, or boosting your confidence with a Roosevelt-style pep talk, your inner dialogue is a versatile and essential part of your psychological toolkit. Embrace your self-talk— it's not only normal but profoundly beneficial. After all, if some of history's greatest minds relied on it, why shouldn't you?

Part V: The Techniques

RJ's Journey through Mindfulness and Self-Talk

RJ's journey through mindfulness and self-talk is a colorful exploration of the mind. Picture RJ diving headfirst into the whirlwind of his thoughts, equipped with nothing but curiosity and a sprinkle of humor. As he learns to step back and observe his internal dialogue without judgment, it's as if he's watching an endless comedy show where unsolicited advice, random musings, and critical voices all take center stage. Part V invites you to join RJ as he discovers the art of simply watching his mental cinema, without needing to jump into any storyline.

Throughout Part V, you'll follow RJ as he masters mindfulness techniques that transform his chaotic thoughts into manageable conversations. From observing his inner dialogues to recognizing patterns in his self-talk, RJ uncovers how certain thoughts can either lift him up or drag him down. You'll gain insights into his strategies for reframing negative thoughts and building resilience. Additionally, delve into the delightful interactions between RJ and Simon the Cockatiel, where their meaningful exchanges serve as unique emotional support. Whether it's through structured journaling or understanding diverse inner voices, this chapter offers a humorous yet profound look at turning inner chaos into harmony.

Armed with scientific knowledge and a newfound appreciation for his chatty brain, RJ decided it was time to refine his self-talk techniques. It was like being a mad scientist, but instead of a laboratory full of bubbling beakers, he had a head full of babbling thoughts. Let's dive into RJ's adventures in 'mastering the art' of talking to himself!

Mindfulness: RJ becoming aware of his selftalk

RJ's first step into the world of mindfulness was like watching a bull try to tiptoe through a china shop – well-intentioned, but initially disastrous.

"Okay, RJ," he said to himself one morning, sitting cross-legged on his living room floor. "Time to be mindful. Just focus on your breath. In... out... in... out... Hey, is that dust bunny shaped like a Java symbol?"

Refocusing his attention, RJ tried again. "Breathe in... breathe out... Hey, remember that bug you couldn't fix yesterday? Maybe if you tried..."

Groaning in frustration, RJ realized that being mindful of his thoughts was harder than he'd anticipated. His mind was like a hyperactive puppy, constantly chasing after new ideas and random observations.

Determined to improve, RJ decided to try a mindfulness app. The soothing voice guided him:

"Notice your thoughts as they arise, like clouds floating across the sky."

"Clouds, got it," RJ muttered. "Oh look, that thought-cloud looks like a computer. And that one's definitely a coffee cup. Ooh, and that one's the blue screen of death. Wait, why are all my thought-clouds computer-related? Am I in the Matrix?"

Despite the rocky start, RJ persevered. Slowly but surely, he began to distinguish between his various inner voices – the critic, the cheerleader, the random fact generator, and the one that was obsessed with whether or not hot dogs could be classified as sandwiches.

As he became more aware of his self-talk, RJ started to notice patterns. His inner critic tended to pipe up when he was tired or stressed, while his cheerleader was loudest after his third cup of coffee.

"Fascinating," RJ mused. "It's like I've got an entire sitcom cast in my head. Wonder if I can get them to reenact Friends episodes during boring meetings?"In the bustling world of RJ, mindfulness became a pivotal tool in understanding his self-talk. Imagine standing amidst a whirlwind of thoughts, each dragging you in different directions, and suddenly realizing that you have the power to step back and just observe without being swept away. This was RJ's first lesson: learning to observe and identify internal dialogue without judgment.

Observing one's own thoughts can initially feel like trying to catch a runaway train. RJ found himself constantly critiquing the snippets of conversations running through his mind, but mindfulness taught him a unique trick - to simply watch without engaging. He started by setting aside a few minutes each day to sit quietly and let his thoughts flow freely. It was as if he became a spectator at an endless mental cinema, watching scenes play out without the need to jump into any storyline. RJ discovered that internal dialogue can be quite bizarre, like a comedy show where unsolicited advice and random musings make up most of the script.

As RJ continued this practice, he began recognizing patterns in his self-talk that significantly affected his emotional well-being. Some days, he felt like a superhero ready to conquer the world; other times, he felt more like a sidekick doubting every move. By noticing these patterns, RJ saw how certain thoughts could either lift his spirits or drain his energy. For instance, every time he thought about a new project, a critical inner voice would whisper, "What if you fail?" Recognizing this pattern was enlightening because it allowed RJ to see how often he sabotaged his own enthusiasm even before getting started.

To combat these negative influences, RJ focused on developing skills to stay present and attentive to current experiences. Instead of dwelling on past mistakes or fretting over future uncertainties, he practiced grounding techniques. Simple things, really, like feeling the texture of his coffee mug in the morning or taking deliberate breaths and paying attention to their rhythm. These small acts turned out to be powerful anchors, helping RJ stay rooted in the present moment rather than drifting off into a sea of worries.

But staying attentive is easier said than done, especially when life feels like an ever-accelerating treadmill. This is where mindfulness techniques such as meditation came into play for RJ. Meditation seemed daunting at first—sitting still with eyes closed conjured images of monks on mountaintops, far removed from RJ's reality. However, he embraced a more accessible approach. Guided meditations for beginners became his best friends. He started with short, five-minute sessions focusing on breathing. As days passed, he extended these sessions, and soon, meditation became his daily mental hygiene routine.

RJ's journey through mindfulness didn't end there; in fact, it opened new avenues for exploring his self-talk further. Mindfulness painted each of his internal voices with distinct colors and personalities. It wasn't just about hearing a critical tone or a supportive one; it was about recognizing the entire spectrum of his internal dialogues. RJ learned that some voices stemmed from childhood experiences, societal expectations, or recent events—all influencing his mindset in various ways.

With increased awareness, RJ began implementing strategies to reframe his thoughts. When a self-doubting voice chimed in, he countered with facts. "What if you fail?" could be met with, "I've succeeded in similar challenges before." These mindful adjustments helped RJ build resilience, allowing him to navigate through doubts and fears with greater ease.

Moreover, RJ noticed that extending mindfulness beyond his internal chatter had a delightful effect on his interactions with others. Conversations became richer as he truly listened without forming immediate judgments. This not only improved his relationships but also provided fresh perspectives that enriched his own self-talk.

One can't overlook the importance of humor in RJ's process. He named his critical inner voice "Skeptical Sam" and his encouraging voice "Cheerful Charlie." Giving them personas added an element of playful detachment, making it easier to handle criticism and praise alike. "Oh, Skeptical Sam is at it again," he'd chuckle, deflating the negativity with lightheartedness.

RJ's exploration didn't stop with personal reflection alone. He took to journaling his experiences, capturing the ebb and flow of his selftalk. Writing served as a mirror, reflecting patterns that were otherwise hard to catch in real-time. Journaling became a companion activity to his mindfulness practices, reinforcing his journey towards better understanding and managing his self-talk.

In essence, mindfulness was a game-changer for RJ. Observing internal dialogues without judgment, recognizing patterns affecting emotional well-being, staying present, and using meditative practices all played crucial roles. Through these steps, RJ transformed his chaotic mental landscape into a more manageable, insight-rich journey—a journey where he became the mindful master of his own thoughts.

Reframing: RJ turning negative self-talk into positive

With his newfound awareness, RJ realized that some of his self-talk wasn't exactly winning any motivational speaker awards. It was time for some serious reframing.

RJ's first attempt at reframing came during a particularly challenging coding session:

Negative thought: "You're an idiot. You'll never figure this out."

RJ's reframe: "Okay, let's try that again. You're not an idiot, you're just... cognitively adventurous! Yeah, that's it. You're not struggling, you're embarking on a thrilling neural expedition!"

While his reframes started out a bit... creative, RJ gradually got better at turning his negative self-talk into more positive and realistic statements.

During a team meeting where he had to present a project update, RJ caught himself thinking, "They're all going to laugh at how little progress you've made."

Taking a deep breath, he reframed: "The team will appreciate my honesty about the challenges, and we can brainstorm solutions together."

To his surprise, the meeting went well. His teammates were indeed understanding and offered helpful suggestions.

"Well, I'll be," RJ thought. "This reframing thing might not be total hogwash after all."

Encouraged, RJ began to approach his reframing with gusto, sometimes getting a bit carried away:

Original thought: "I'm going to be late for work."

RJ's reframe: "I'm not late; I'm giving the universe an opportunity to miss me and appreciate me more when I arrive!"

His boss was less than impressed with this particular reframe, but RJ's enthusiasm for positive self-talk remained undeterred.In RJ's journey to transform his negative self-perceptions into positive outlooks, one of the first steps is identifying common negative selftalk phrases and understanding their impact. RJ would often catch himself saying things like, "I'm not good enough," "I'll never get this right," or "Why even bother trying?" These phrases might seem harmless or even motivational in a twisted way, but more often than not, they create a cycle of self-doubt and negativity. This internal dialogue can significantly affect one's self-esteem and overall mental health. RJ realized that these negative statements were not just casual thoughts; they were shaping his reality.

Once RJ identified these detrimental phrases, he needed techniques for counteracting them with positive affirmations. This was no easy task. It's like wrestling a sumo wrestler made of pessimism! However, RJ began practicing by replacing negative thoughts with positive ones. For instance, instead of thinking, "I can't do this," he started saying, "I am capable, and I can learn how to do this." It felt awkward at first, like wearing mismatched socks, but over time, these positive affirmations became more natural.

The process of cognitive restructuring played a crucial role in shifting RJ's perspective. Cognitive restructuring involves challenging the underlying assumptions behind negative thoughts. For example, when RJ caught himself thinking, "I'll never be successful," he asked himself, "Is there any real evidence for this belief?" Often, there wasn't any solid evidence, just fear and anxiety. By examining these thoughts critically, he managed to dismantle them piece by piece, replacing them with more balanced and realistic beliefs. This practice takes patience (and maybe a little bit of stubbornness), but it's essential for breaking free from recurring negative cycles.

Building resilience through regular positive thinking exercises was another cornerstone of RJ's transformation. Think of it like going to the gym, but for your brain. Just as muscles grow stronger with consistent exercise, so does one's ability to maintain a positive outlook. RJ adopted several exercises into his daily routine. One of his favorites was the gratitude journal, where each day he noted down three things he was grateful for. At first, it seemed cheesy, but RJ quickly noticed a shift in his focus—from what was going wrong to what was going right. He also employed visualization techniques, imagining successful outcomes instead of failures. This mental rehearsal helped build confidence and reduced anxiety about future events.

Additionally, RJ learned to engage in conversations with himself that were constructive rather than destructive. He personified his inner critic, giving it a name and an identity. This allowed him to separate himself from his negative thoughts and address them directly. When this critical voice popped up, RJ would envision having a talk with it, almost like a debate. "Okay, Negative Nelly," he'd say, "What's your point? And why should I believe you?" This practice made it easier to dismiss the negativity and replace it with something more uplifting.

Practicing mindfulness-based techniques also contributed significantly to RJ's journey. Although he wasn't always comfortable sitting still like a monk, RJ found value in short mindfulness practices that helped him stay grounded. Simple activities, like focusing on his breath, taking mindful walks, or even paying attention to the texture of a stress ball, allowed RJ to step back from his thoughts and view them more objectively. This distance made it easier to identify and challenge negative self-talk.

RJ also leaned heavily on social support networks. While it's important to develop personal strategies for combating negative self-talk, sharing experiences with friends or a supportive community can provide additional strength. RJ often discussed his thoughts with a close friend, who would offer a fresh perspective and sometimes even find humor in RJ's overblown worries. Laughing at oneself occasionally can be powerful; it lightens the emotional load and helps put things into perspective.

RS, In addition, engaging in meaningful interactions with Simon the Cockatiel, operated as a unique form of emotional support for RJ. The simple acts of talking to Simon or observing his playful antics served as a distraction from negative thoughts and reminded RJ of the joys of living in the moment. These moments contributed to building a positive mindset by providing daily doses of joy and companionship.

Throughout this journey, RJ understood that transforming negative self-perceptions isn't about flipping a switch but rather turning a gradual dial. It involves not only developing new habits and thought patterns but also nurturing them consistently over time. Sure, there were days when RJ slipped back into old habits, but with each slip, he grew more adept at catching himself sooner and steering his thoughts back on track.

Dialogic Self-Theory: RJ exploring multiple inner voices

As RJ delved deeper into self-talk techniques, he stumbled upon the concept of Dialogic Self-Theory. The idea that he could have multiple inner "selves" in dialogue with each other was like discovering he had his own internal improv troupe.

"Ladies and gentlemen," RJ announced to his empty living room, "welcome to 'Whose Line of Code Is It Anyway?' – the show where everything's made up and the points don't matter!" RJ began to identify and name his various inner voices:

Logic Lad: The voice of reason and analytical thinking.

Worry Wally: The anxious voice always forecasting doom and gloom.

Creative Carl: The out-of-the-box thinker with sometimes questionable ideas.

Motivated Mary: The inner cheerleader always ready with a pep talk.

With this cast of characters in mind, RJ's internal dialogues became much more entertaining:

Logic Lad: "We should start this project by outlining the main objectives."

Worry Wally: "But what if we forget something crucial? We'll fail miserably!"

Creative Carl: "Hey, what if we present the whole thing as a musical? Code: The Broadway Debugger!"

Motivated Mary: "That's the spirit! We can do anything we set our minds to!"

Logic Lad: "...Let's table the musical idea for now."

While these internal discussions were amusing, RJ found that they actually helped him consider different perspectives and make more balanced decisions. Plus, it made boring tasks a lot more entertaining.When it comes to understanding the Dialogic SelfTheory, you might feel like you're suddenly part of an animated conversation in your own head. Imagine a room full of people, each with their distinct voice and personality. These inner voices can range from supportive cheerleaders to overly critical coaches. Welcome to RJ's world of multiple inner voices! In exploring this concept, we uncover some fascinating insights into how our minds work.

First, let's dive into understanding these multiple inner voices and their roles. You know those moments when you're deciding whether to have that extra slice of cake, and a little voice says, "Go for it! You've earned it!" while another sternly adds, "Think of your diet!" These voices are not some quirky character trait but rather an integral part of our psyche. They represent different facets of our identity, shaped by our experiences, beliefs, and emotions. RJ noticed he had a practical voice urging him to plan, a nostalgic one reminiscing about the past, and even a daring voice pushing him to take risks. By recognizing these voices, RJ started to understand the rich tapestry of his inner world.

Now, how do these diverse self-voices contribute to personal conflict or harmony? Think about a group project where everyone has strong opinions. If they communicate well, they create something magnificent; if not, chaos ensues. Our inner voices are no different. When these voices clash, it can lead to internal strife. For instance, RJ often found himself conflicted between his pragmatic and adventurous selves, causing stress and indecision. However, when his voices aligned, such as his nurturing voice supporting his goaloriented side, he experienced a sense of peace and purpose. Recognizing this dynamic helped RJ navigate through his mental landscape more harmoniously.

So, what techniques did RJ use to identify and engage with these diverse inner perspectives? One effective method involved listening actively. RJ would sit in a quiet place, tune into his thoughts, and note which "voice" was speaking. It sounds simple, but it requires patience and practice. He also used visualization, imagining his inner voices as characters with distinct appearances and mannerisms. This made it easier for him to separate them and understand their influences. Moreover, RJ kept a journal, jotting down dialogues between his various voices. Writing these interactions helped him see patterns and gain clarity about his inner conflicts.

Inner dialogues became a tool for fostering self-understanding and growth. Rather than dismissing or fighting his critical voice, RJ started engaging with it compassionately. He would ask why it felt the need to be so harsh and what fears underpinned its criticisms. Through this process, he discovered underlying insecurities and unmet needs that needed addressing. For example, his critical voice often stemmed from a fear of failure, rooted in past experiences. By acknowledging and addressing these fears, RJ could reframe his inner dialogue to be more supportive and constructive.

RJ's journey with the Dialogic Self-Theory illustrated the profound impact of inner dialogues on personal growth. By becoming aware of his multiple inner voices, he could better navigate his thoughts and emotions. Instead of being overwhelmed by conflicting perspectives, he learned to mediate between them, creating a more balanced and harmonious inner world. This shift not only improved his mental well-being but also enhanced his decision-making and interpersonal relationships.

Written Dialogue: RJ using journaling as a form of structured self-talk

Inspired by his success with internal dialogues, RJ decided to take things a step further by journaling. It was time to give his inner voices some ink.

Not Harley Ink - Pen to Paper ink!

RJ's first journaling attempt looked something like this:

Dear Diary,

Today I debugged a particularly nasty piece of code. It was like trying to untangle earbuds that had been in a pocket with keys and loose change – in a washing machine.

Logic Lad says: "The systematic approach we took was effective."

Worry Wally says: "But what if we missed something? The code could explode!"

Creative Carl says: "Can code explode? That would be cool. Explosive Code: The Next Big Thing in Tech!"

Motivated Mary says: "Whether it explodes or not, we'll handle it like champs!"

Note to self: Maybe lay off the coffee before journaling next time.

As he continued his journaling practice, RJ found it incredibly helpful for processing his thoughts and emotions. He even started carrying a small notebook with him, jotting down insights and amusing internal dialogues throughout the day.

This habit led to some interesting moments, like when he was furiously scribbling in his notebook during a team meeting. His colleague leaned over and whispered, "Taking detailed notes, huh? That's so diligent of you!"

If only they knew he was transcribing a heated debate between Logic Lad and Creative Carl about whether it was possible to code a program that could predict the perfect time to microwave popcorn without burning it.Journaling, often seen as scribbling in a notebook or tapping away on a digital device, can actually be a powerful tool for guiding and structuring self-talk. RJ discovered this firsthand during his journey through mindfulness and self-awareness. Writing provides an outlet for thoughts and feelings that might otherwise remain tangled in the mind. By putting pen to paper, RJ found he could clarify his thoughts, making it easier to understand and manage them.

One of the key benefits of journaling is its ability to provide a safe space for expressing emotions without judgment. For RJ, it was like having a private therapist available 24/7. Whether he felt anger, sadness, joy, or confusion, writing allowed him to release these emotions constructively. This practice not only helped in reducing stress but also in gaining insights into his emotional patterns.

However, it's not just about free-writing whatever comes to mind. To address specific self-talk issues, structured journaling methods can be incredibly effective. RJ experimented with various techniques to address his inner dialogue. For example, he would set aside time each day to write down his negative thoughts and then challenge them by asking questions such as, "Is this thought based on facts or assumptions?" or "What evidence do I have that contradicts this belief?" This exercise helped RJ reframe his negative self-talk and develop a more balanced perspective.

Another method RJ found useful was the "ABC" technique: Activating event, Belief, Consequence. Whenever RJ experienced a distressing event, he would jot it down (A), identify the underlying belief (B), and note the consequence of that belief (C). By doing so, he could see the direct impact of his beliefs on his emotions and behaviors. This clarity empowered him to modify his beliefs, leading to healthier self-talk and improved emotional well-being.

To explore various self-voices, RJ used specific prompts and exercises. One effective exercise involved personifying different aspects of himself. He gave names to his inner critic, inner cheerleader, and even his inner sage. This way, he could engage in dialogues between these voices, understanding their perspectives and finding ways to mediate conflicts. Prompts like "What does my inner critic say about this situation?" followed by "How would my inner cheerleader respond?" provided RJ with valuable insights and encouraged self-compassion.

Additionally, RJ tried the "Stream of Consciousness" writing where he wrote continuously for a set period without worrying about grammar or coherence. This unfiltered writing often revealed subconscious thoughts and feelings. By reviewing these entries later, RJ could identify recurring themes and address them more effectively.

Journaling also offered long-term benefits for RJ's mental health. Consistent practice helped him to track his progress over time, celebrate small victories, and acknowledge areas needing improvement. RJ noticed that on days he skipped journaling, his self-talk tended to revert to old, unhelpful patterns. This prompted him to make journaling a non-negotiable part of his daily routine.

The power of consistent journaling lies in its ability to build selfdiscipline and foster a sense of accountability. By maintaining a regular journaling habit, RJ developed greater self-awareness and emotional resilience. He was better equipped to handle life's ups and downs, as he could rely on his journal to process his thoughts and emotions constructively.

Moreover, the act of writing itself became a form of meditation for RJ. It allowed him to slow down, reflect, and become more present.

In today's fast-paced world, taking a few minutes each day to journal can serve as a much-needed pause button, providing mental clarity and peace.

Overall, RJ's journey with journaling illustrates how this simple yet powerful tool can guide and structure self-talk. By using writing as an outlet, employing structured methods, exploring various selfvoices through prompts, and committing to a consistent practice, RJ was able to transform his relationship with his inner dialogue. This ultimately led to improved mental health and a greater sense of wellbeing.

RJ talking bird talk to Simon the Cockatiel

In his quest to master the art of self-talk, RJ stumbled upon an unexpected practice partner – Simon, his newly adopted cockatiel. It turned out that talking to a bird was not that different from talking to himself, except the bird occasionally talked back (mostly to demand crackers and attention).

RJ began including Simon in his self-talk sessions:

"So, Simon, do you think we should use a recursive function here, or would an iterative approach be more efficient?"

Simon's response: "Pretty bird! Cracker!"

"You make an excellent point," RJ nodded sagely. "We should indeed consider the space complexity. And yes, you are a pretty bird."

To RJ's surprise, he found that explaining his thoughts to Simon (or at least, to a Simon-shaped rubber duck) often helped him clarify his ideas and solve problems more effectively.

His colleagues, however, were becoming increasingly concerned about his sanity:

"RJ," his manager approached him cautiously one day, "we couldn't help but notice you've been... talking to your coffee mug a lot lately. And calling it Simon. Is everything okay?"

"Oh, that!" RJ laughed. "Don't worry, I'm not going cuckoo. Well, not more than usual. I'm just practicing rubber duck debugging. You know, explaining the problem to an inanimate object to help solve it? Simon's my rubber duck. Well, rubber bird. Well, actually, he's a real bird, but he's not here, so the mug is his stand-in, and... you know what, never mind. Everything's fine!"

His manager walked away looking more concerned than before, but RJ just shrugged. After all, if talking to an imaginary bird helped him code better, who was he to argue with success?

As RJ continued to explore and refine these techniques, he found that his self-talk was becoming more structured, more positive, and dare he say it, more useful. Sure, he still had moments where his inner voices got a bit carried away (Creative Carl's "underwater coding studio" idea was particularly problematic), but overall, he felt more in control of his internal dialogue.

"Well, team," RJ said to his inner council as he prepared for bed one night, "I'd say we're making progress. Who knew talking to ourselves could be so productive?"

As he drifted off to sleep, RJ couldn't help but smile. His journey into the world of self-talk had been wild, weird, and wonderfully entertaining. And the best part? It was far from over. With his newfound techniques and his trusty inner voices (and Simon), RJ was ready for whatever challenges tomorrow might bring.

"Bring it on, world," he mumbled sleepily. "Me, myself, and I are ready for you. And Simon too, of course."

In his dreams that night, RJ found himself on a game show hosted by Logic Lad, with Worry Wally, Creative Carl, and Motivated Mary as contestants. The challenge? Debug a program while blindfolded and standing on one foot. Strangely enough, it was the most restful sleep he'd had in weeks.Engaging in meaningful communication with a pet can offer immense emotional support. Pets, like Simon the Cockatiel, provide not only companionship but also serve as catalysts for emotional well-being. Understanding the therapeutic benefits of interacting with pets, we discover that they can help reduce stress, alleviate feelings of loneliness, and even improve overall mental health. Research has shown that engaging with pets through activities like talking, petting, or playing can release oxytocin, a hormone associated with bonding and affection. This helps to lower cortisol levels, reducing stress and anxiety.

Techniques for creating bonding activities with pets are essential for fostering these therapeutic benefits. With Simon, RJ could start by setting aside dedicated time each day to interact with him. Engaging Simon in conversations, mimicking his sounds, or even teaching him new words can enhance their bond. Activities such as hand-feeding treats, allowing Simon to perch on RJ's shoulder, or simply spending quiet moments together can build trust and deepen their connection. It's important for RJ to be patient and consistent, recognizing that building a relationship with Simon is a process.

Using pet interaction to reflect on and improve one's own self-talk is another valuable aspect. When RJ talks to Simon, he mirrors his inner dialogue. This interaction allows RJ to become more aware of his thoughts and how they influence his mood. For instance, if RJ tends to speak harshly to himself, he might catch these negative patterns while talking to Simon and consciously reframe them into more positive statements. This practice can be enlightening; as RJ adjusts his tone with Simon, he naturally begins to adjust his selftalk, fostering a kinder and more supportive inner dialogue.

Observing non-verbal communication and its parallels to human self-dialogue provides another layer of understanding. Unlike humans, Simon communicates predominantly through body language and vocalizations. By paying close attention to Simon's cues—such as his posture, feather fluffs, or changes in chirping patterns—RJ can learn the subtleties of non-verbal communication. This observation can teach RJ to be more attuned to his non-verbal signals, such as body tension or facial expressions, which are often linked to his emotional state. Recognizing these signs can help RJ address his feelings more effectively, improving his overall emotional intelligence.

Moreover, RJ could find that the simplicity of communicating with Simon strips away complexities and social judgments, encouraging a more straightforward and genuine form of interaction. Sometimes RJ would have deep and meaningful conversations with Simon in the shower to start his day. Perfect. Pets do not judge; they respond with sincerity, providing a safe space for RJ to express himself freely. This uninhibited communication can be therapeutic, offering RJ a break from overanalyzing his thoughts and fostering a more compassionate self-view.

Final Insights

RJ's journey through mindfulness, reframing his negative self-talk, and understanding multiple inner voices has been a laugh-filled odyssey. Imagine giving your inner critic a zany name like "Skeptical Sam" and treating it like an old cartoon nemesis. RJ transformed these inner dialogues from daunting monologues into engaging character interactions, making them more manageable and even amusing. Journaling became his personal playground for this mental adventure, where writing down doubts and countering them with logic turned his self-doubt into a comedy sketch rather than a tragedy.

Adding Simon the Cockatiel to the mix, RJ found a unique way to lighten the mood and improve his mental well-being. Chatting with Simon, mimicking his chirps, or simply observing his playful antics provided both a break from internal chaos and a lesson in authentic, judgment-free communication. This quirky companionship reminded RJ that sometimes the best way to navigate life's twists and turns is with a bit of humor and a feathered friend by your side. In essence, RJ's story is about turning a seemingly tangled mental landscape into an enjoyable and enlightening journey filled with laughter and unexpected allies.

Part VI: The Philosophical Angle

The Intricacies of RJ's Self-Talk and Its Implications

RJ's self-talk is a fascinating blend of internal dialogue, introspection, and occasional bursts of humor. Picture RJ navigating his day with an ongoing commentary that ranges from motivational pep talks to deep dives into the meaning of life. Part VI further unravels the many layers of RJ's self-talk, exploring how these internal conversations influence everything from his decision-making to his emotional well-being.

You'll soon discover how the frequency and quality of RJ's self-talk play a crucial role in his journey toward deeper self-awareness. Is he just chattering away about mundane tasks, or is there more going on? By examining the intricacies of RJ's internal narrative, we delve into the fine line between casual musings and profound cognitive reflection. Expect to uncover the ways in which RJ's verbalized thoughts act as a mirror to his psyche, revealing hidden triggers and personal insights. So buckle up and get ready to dive into RJ's mind, where every word counts and self-discovery awaits!

As RJ delved deeper into his self-talk journey, he found himself venturing into unexpected territory - the realm of philosophy. It was like he'd accidentally wandered into a tweed-jacket-filled seminar while looking for the snack machine, but now that he was here, he might as well grab a pipe and ponder the nature of existence.

Self-Reflection: Is RJ's Increased Self-Talk a Sign of Deeper Introspection?

One lazy Sunday afternoon, as RJ was engaged in a heated debate with himself about whether a hotdog was a sandwich (Creative Carl was all for it, while Logic Lad demanded stricter sandwich classifications), he had a sudden realization.

"Wait a minute," he said out loud, causing Simon the cockatiel to startle. "Am I becoming... philosophical?"

The thought was both exciting and mildly terrifying, like realizing you might have superpowers, but they're really inconvenient ones like the ability to always know when someone's talking about you, but only if they're on another continent.

RJ decided to lean into this new development. He put on his most contemplative expression (which mostly involved squinting and stroking his non-existent beard) and addressed his reflection in the mirror:

"Oh wise and handsome RJ," he intoned, "is this increased self-talk a sign of deeper introspection? Or just a sign that I really need to get out more?"

His reflection, unsurprisingly, offered no answers. But the question lingered in RJ's mind like a persistent pop-up ad for enlightenment.

He began to notice that his self-talk had indeed taken on a more introspective quality. Instead of just debating the merits of different coding languages or rehearsing conversations with his rubber duck debugger, he found himself pondering deeper questions:

"Why do I code? Is it just to pay the bills, or am I seeking to create order in a chaotic digital world? And why did I choose to learn Python instead of Ruby? Was it a rational decision, or was I subconsciously influenced by my childhood love of snakes?"

His colleagues at work started to notice a change too. During lunch breaks, instead of his usual chatter about the latest tech gadgets, RJ could be found staring pensively into his sandwich, muttering things like:

"If I eat this sandwich, do I become one with the sandwich? Or does the sandwich become one with me? Are we all just cosmic sandwiches in the lunch box of existence?"

His coworker Jim finally broke the silence: "Uh, RJ? You okay there, buddy? You've been staring at that tuna on rye for ten minutes."

RJ looked up, a bit startled. "Oh, yes, quite alright. Just contemplating the metaphysical implications of lunch consumption. You know, normal Tuesday stuff."

As RJ continued to explore this newfound introspective side, he couldn't help but wonder if he was onto something profound, or if he had just discovered a very convoluted form of procrastination. Either way, it was certainly making his internal monologues more interesting.Understanding whether RJ's increased self-talk signals deeper introspection begins with examining the frequency and content of his self-dialogue. This aspect offers a window into RJ's mental processes, much like eavesdropping on someone's inner conversations can hint at their state of mind. When RJ talks to himself more often than usual, we have to wonder if he's just really excited about something or if he's delving into deeper layers of thought.

The sheer number of self-directed conversations RJ engages in might seem trivial at first glance—after all, who doesn't chat to themselves now and then? But when this habit becomes frequent, it suggests a constant need for self-analysis. Imagine RJ constantly reviewing his decisions, questioning his beliefs, or replaying events in his head. These scenarios illustrate a deeper engagement with his thoughts and feelings rather than merely verbalizing mundane tasks.

Shifting our focus from quantity to quality, the nature of RJ's selftalk is equally revealing. If RJ's internal monologue comprises critical evaluations, reflections on personal experiences, or inquiries into his motives, these elements indicate a level of self-analysis that goes beyond surface chatter. It is as if RJ is holding a mirror up to his psyche, scrutinizing each part for clarity and understanding. For example, RJ may find himself pondering why he reacted angrily in a particular situation, dissecting his emotions piece by piece to uncover underlying triggers.

Self-talk does more than just serve as a diagnostic tool for selfanalysis—it actively contributes to RJ's understanding of his emotions and thoughts. Verbalizing these inner experiences allows individuals like RJ to externalize and thus better comprehend their feelings. Think of it as trying to explain a complicated concept out loud; sometimes, hearing the words helps the speaker understand the idea better. Similarly, when RJ speaks to himself about feeling overwhelmed, he might recognize patterns or root causes that weren't apparent before.

This process of verbalization leads us to the next point: the link between articulating inner experiences and gaining personal insights. Once RJ starts putting his feelings and thoughts into words, he opens the door for new perspectives. It's akin to keeping a diary where capturing emotions on paper can reveal hidden aspects of oneself. For instance, RJ might discover that his repeated worries about work stem from an unacknowledged fear of failure. By voicing these concerns, even internally, RJ gains the insight needed to address them constructively.

Casual self-talk often evolves into structured cognitive reflection, marking another step toward deeper introspection. While initially, RJ's self-talk might be spontaneous and unplanned—akin to chatting with a friend about random topics—it gradually transforms into more deliberate and organized forms of reflection. Picture RJ walking through a park, initially making offhand comments about the scenery but soon engaging in a focused dialogue on life's bigger questions. This shift indicates that RJ is not just talking to himself for company but is using the conversation as a cognitive tool for deeper reflection.

An interesting facet of this transformation lies in how structured self-talk can enhance cognitive insights. Imagine RJ preparing to face a challenging task. His casual remarks about the difficulty might evolve into a systematic analysis of potential strategies, advantages, and pitfalls. As RJ structures his thoughts more coherently, he is likely to arrive at more profound conclusions and innovative solutions.

Thus, we see that RJ's increased self-talk does indeed signify deeper introspection. Through frequent and meaningful self-analysis, understanding emotions and thoughts, verbalizing inner experiences, and transforming casual self-talk into structured reflection, RJ embarks on a journey of self-discovery. Each element of his internal dialogue serves as a building block, contributing to a fuller, richer sense of self-awareness and personal insight.

Consciousness and Self: The Role of Internal Dialogue in Self-Awareness

As RJ's philosophical musings deepened, he found himself grappling with questions of consciousness and self-awareness. It was like his brain had decided to host its own TED talk, but forgot to invite an actual expert, so RJ had to fill in with his best imitation of a profound thinker.

One morning, while brushing his teeth, RJ had a startling thought:

"If I talk to myself, and I listen to myself... who's doing the talking, and who's doing the listening?"

This sent him into a spiral of existential wonder, toothbrush dangling forgotten from his mouth as he stared wide-eyed at his reflection.

"Am I the voice in my head? Or am I the one listening to the voice? Or am I some third entity, observing both the talker and the listener? Is this what it feels like to be a one-man podcast?"

RJ's exploration of consciousness led to some interesting experiments. He tried to catch his thoughts before they formed into words, which mostly resulted in him looking constipated as he concentrated intensely on the contents of his own mind.

He also attempted to observe his dreams, leaving sticky notes all over his bedroom that said "YOU'RE DREAMING!" in big letters. This backfired spectacularly when he groggily got up for a glass of water in the middle of the night, saw the notes, and spent the next hour trying to fly and walk through walls before realizing he was, in fact, very much awake.

RJ's pondering on self-awareness reached new heights (or perhaps new depths) when he tried to examine his own process of selfexamination:

"I'm aware that I'm aware of being aware... but am I aware of being aware of being aware of being aware?"

This linguistic loop sent him into a dizzy spell, and he had to sit down and have a stern talk with himself about the dangers of recursive self-awareness.

Despite the occasional mental acrobatics, RJ found that paying attention to his internal dialogue did increase his self-awareness. He became more attuned to his thoughts and emotions, noticing patterns he hadn't seen before.

"Fascinating," he mused one day. "It seems that my productivity is inversely proportional to the number of cat videos I've watched. Who would have thought?"

This newfound self-awareness even extended to his coding habits. RJ realized that his best work happened when his internal dialogue was a balance of focused problem-solving and creative tangents. Too much Logic Lad, and his code became dry and uninspired. Too much Creative Carl, and he'd end up with a program that tried to translate binary into interpretive dance.

As RJ continued to explore the connection between his internal dialogue and his sense of self, he couldn't shake the feeling that he was on the brink of some great revelation. Or possibly a nervous breakdown. It was hard to tell sometimes.Internal dialogue plays a fundamental role in fostering self-awareness. When RJ engages in self-talk, they are essentially holding a mirror up to their thoughts and emotions. This reflection is pivotal for self-monitoring and regulation. Think of internal dialogue as an ongoing conversation with oneself, where one can evaluate actions, decisions, and experiences in real time. By regularly checking in with their inner voice, RJ becomes more attuned to their feelings and reactions.

Imagine RJ facing a challenging situation at work. Through self-talk, they might evaluate the event by asking themselves questions like, "Why am I feeling so frustrated?" or "How can I handle this better next time?" This kind of internal questioning helps RJ identify specific triggers and responses, allowing them to devise strategies for managing similar situations in the future. Over time, regular selfmonitoring through internal dialogue becomes a habit, leading to enhanced emotional regulation and better decision-making.

The impact of self-talk on evolving one's identity and consciousness cannot be understated. Our internal dialogue significantly influences how we perceive ourselves and our place in the world. For RJ, talking to themselves isn't just about narrating daily activities; it's a powerful mechanism for shaping their beliefs, values, and ultimately, their identity. When RJ repeatedly tells themselves they are capable and resilient, these affirmations solidify into core aspects of their personality.

Consider the concept of neuroplasticity—the brain's ability to reorganize itself by forming new neural connections. Internal dialogue acts as a tool to reinforce positive thoughts and behaviors.

When RJ consciously chooses to replace negative self-talk with encouraging words, they are literally reshaping their mind. This transformation doesn't happen overnight, but consistent practice gradually alters RJ's sense of self, enhancing their confidence and outlook on life.

Distinguishing between conscious and subconscious self-dialogue is another vital aspect of understanding internal dialogue. Conscious self-talk involves deliberate, thoughtful communication with oneself. It's the type of dialogue RJ can recall and reflect upon, such as planning their day or giving themselves a pep talk before a presentation. In contrast, subconscious self-dialogue occurs beneath the surface of conscious awareness, influencing RJ's thoughts and behaviors without them even realizing it.

For example, RJ might have a deeply ingrained belief that they're not good enough—a notion planted in their subconscious from past experiences. This belief might manifest in subtle ways, such as hesitation to take on new challenges or an automatic assumption of failure. By bringing these subconscious dialogues to light through conscious self-examination, RJ has the opportunity to challenge and rewrite these narratives.

Reflective thought plays a crucial role in developing a coherent sense of self. When RJ takes time to ponder their internal dialogue, they're engaging in a deeper level of introspection. Reflective thought involves analyzing their thoughts, feelings, and actions to gain insights into who they are and what drives them. This process is akin to assembling pieces of a puzzle—each reflection adds a piece, gradually revealing a clearer picture of RJ's true self.

One effective method RJ might use is journaling. By writing down their thoughts and reviewing them periodically, RJ can track their emotional and psychological growth. Patterns start to emerge, highlighting areas where they've made progress and others where they still struggle. This continuous cycle of reflection and adjustment allows RJ to refine their self-perception and align their actions with their values more consistently.

A practical guideline for utilizing internal dialogue effectively is to practice mindfulness. Mindfulness involves being fully present in the moment and observing one's thoughts without judgment. For RJ, adopting a mindful approach to self-talk means acknowledging their inner dialogue, whether positive or negative, and understanding its impact on their well-being.

By simply noticing when they engage in self-criticism or self-praise, RJ gains insight into their habitual thinking patterns. This heightened awareness is the first step toward transforming unhelpful self-dialogues into constructive ones. A mindfulness exercise could involve RJ setting aside a few minutes each day to sit quietly, focus on their breath, and observe their thoughts as they arise. Over time, this practice helps RJ cultivate a more compassionate and supportive inner voice.

Language and Thought: How Verbalization Shapes RJ's Thinking

As RJ delved deeper into his self-talk exploration, he began to notice how the very act of putting his thoughts into words was shaping his thinking process. It was like his brain had discovered a new toy language - and was now intent on using it to build elaborate castles of thought, complete with moats of metaphor and drawbridges of deduction.

One day, while working on a particularly tricky bit of code, RJ found himself narrating his problem-solving process out loud:

"Okay, so if we initialize the variable here, then loop through the array, checking each element against our condition..."

Suddenly, he paused, a look of wonder spreading across his face. "Hold the phone," he muttered. "Am I thinking in code? Has my brain been compiled into a programming language?"

This realization led RJ down a rabbit hole of linguistic contemplation. He began to notice how the words he used in his selftalk influenced his perception and problem-solving approaches.

When he framed a coding challenge as a "battle" against bugs, he found himself taking a more aggressive, brute-force approach to debugging. But when he described the same task as a "puzzle" to be solved, his tactics became more methodical and creative.

Intrigued by this discovery, RJ decided to experiment with different linguistic frameworks in his self-talk. He tried thinking about his code in terms of cooking recipes:

"First, we'll marinate the data in a robust algorithm sauce, then we'll sauté the variables until they're nice and crispy..."

To his surprise, this culinary-coding fusion actually led to some innovative solutions, although it did make him inexplicably hungry every time he opened his IDE.

RJ's linguistic adventures didn't stop at work. He began to notice how the words he used in his internal dialogue affected his mood and behavior in everyday life. When he caught himself thinking, "This day is a disaster," he'd consciously rephrase it to something like, "This day is a thrilling obstacle course of unexpected challenges!"

His coworkers were somewhat baffled by his newfound optimism:

"RJ," his manager said one day, "the coffee machine is broken, the server's down, and a pigeon somehow got into the office and is now nesting in the ficus. How can you possibly be smiling?"

RJ grinned. "Ah, but think of it as an exciting opportunity to expand our problem-solving skills, test our adaptability, and connect with nature in the workplace!"

His manager stared at him for a long moment before slowly backing away, muttering something about HR and mandatory vacation days.

As RJ continued to explore the interplay between language and thought, he couldn't help but wonder about the limits of this relationship. Could he think thoughts that he couldn't put into words? Were there ideas lurking in the non-verbal realms of his mind, waiting for the right language to give them form?

These ponderings led to some interesting late-night experiments:

"What if I try to think without words?" RJ mused. "I'll just sit here and experience pure, unadulterated thought!"

Thirty seconds later:

"Nope, still thinking in words. Although I did get a brief mental image of a tap-dancing giraffe. Not sure what that means, but I'm counting it as a win for non-verbal cognition!"

Despite the occasional bout of mental gymnastics, RJ found that being more conscious of his internal language was genuinely improving his thinking processes. His code became more elegant, his problem-solving more creative, and his dad jokes... well, they were still terrible, but now they were terribly self-aware.When diving into the mind of RJ and his intricate self-talk, we must first understand how verbalization influences his cognitive processes. Language development and complex thought patterns are tightly interwoven. It's almost like they've been best friends since childhood, constantly playing off each other. In RJ's case, it's like having a running commentary in his head that shapes his thinking.

As RJ articulates his thoughts, he experiences clearer reasoning and enhanced problem-solving abilities. Have you ever tried solving a complicated math problem silently? Sometimes, all you need to do is say it out loud for it to make sense. For RJ, voicing his thoughts acts as a mental filter, clarifying issues and spotlighting solutions. This isn't just about vocalizing ideas but also about mentally phrasing them. By turning abstract thoughts into concrete words, RJ can dissect and analyze them more effectively.

Self-talk plays a crucial role in organizing RJ's mental processes and memory. Think of it as a neatly arranged closet versus one where everything is thrown in haphazardly. When RJ speaks to himself, he categorizes his thoughts, making it easier to retrieve information when needed. It's like creating mental folders; each piece of information has its place. This organized structure helps RJ connect dots he might have otherwise missed, leading to deeper insights and better decision-making.

But what happens when RJ changes the language he uses in his selftalk? Imagine swapping out gloomy clouds for sunny skies. The power of positive or negative wording can drastically alter perspectives and decisions. If RJ consistently tells himself, "I can't do this," guess what? He probably won't. But if he shifts to saying, "I've got this!" his mindset changes, opening doors to possibilities he hadn't considered.

By consciously modifying his inner dialogue, RJ can challenge unhelpful beliefs and replace them with constructive ones. It's not just about being your own cheerleader—though having pep talks with yourself certainly doesn't hurt. This shift in language can transform doubt into confidence, hesitation into action, and confusion into clarity.

RJ's self-talk also serves as a rehearsal space, where he preps for real-life interactions and decisions. Picture him as an actor running through lines before the big performance. By discussing scenarios in his mind, he prepares himself for various outcomes. This preparatory self-talk boosts his readiness and resilience, reducing anxiety and improving overall performance.

Language doesn't just shape RJ's current thinking patterns; it also influences how he stores and recalls memories. Suppose RJ repeatedly frames an event positively when recollecting it. In that case, his brain starts associating that memory with positive emotions, reinforcing a beneficial outlook on past experiences. Conversely, negative framing can anchor him in feelings of regret or anger, affecting his future interactions and perceptions.

Shifting gears slightly, let's reflect on the importance of context in RJ's self-talk. The environment and circumstances often dictate the tone and content of his internal dialogue. For instance, during stressful times, RJ's self-talk may lean towards survival mode, focusing on immediate problems rather than long-term goals. Conversely, in a relaxed setting, his self-talk becomes more reflective and open-ended, allowing for creative and strategic thinking.

Recognizing these contextual shifts empowers RJ to tailor his selftalk to be more adaptive. He learns to harness productive selfdialogue during crises while fostering innovative thinking during calmer periods. This adaptability becomes a crucial tool in navigating life's complexities and uncertainties.

It's fascinating how self-talk isn't just a solitary activity. Social interactions and feedback loops play significant roles. RJ's self-talk often mirrors conversations he has had with others or anticipates future dialogues. This mirroring helps him process social cues and expectations, refining his responses and behaviors accordingly. It also allows RJ to experiment with different viewpoints, ultimately enriching his understanding of diverse perspectives.

Let's not forget humor – an essential ingredient in RJ's self-talk recipe. A light-hearted approach to internal dialogue can diffuse tension and prevent overthinking. Poking fun at oneself or finding humor in tough situations provides relief and creates a balanced perspective. RJ's ability to laugh at his quirks and missteps fosters a healthier relationship with himself, promoting resilience and emotional well-being.

Ultimately, RJ's self-talk is a dynamic interplay of verbalization, cognitive processes, and emotional regulation. It's not merely about talking to oneself but engaging in a continuous dialogue that shapes thoughts, organizes memories, and guides decisions. By understanding and optimizing this internal conversation, RJ unlocks new levels of introspection, self-awareness, and personal growth.

The Inner Narrator: Are We All Constantly Telling Our Own Story?

As RJ's journey into the philosophical implications of self-talk continued, he stumbled upon a particularly intriguing question: Was he constantly narrating his own life story?

The thought hit him one day as he was making his morning coffee, a process which had somehow turned into an internal monologue worthy of a nature documentary:

"Here we see the wild programmer in his natural habitat, embarking on the daily ritual of caffeine acquisition. Watch as he skillfully measures the grounds, his movements honed by years of evolution and a desperate need not to fall asleep at his keyboard."

RJ paused, coffee scoop halfway to the machine. "Wait a minute," he said aloud, causing Simon the cockatiel to cock his head curiously. "Am I narrating my own life? Have I become the Morgan Freeman of my own existence?"

This realization sent RJ into a spiral of self-awareness. He began to notice how often he was mentally narrating his actions, thoughts, and experiences. It was as if his brain had decided to star in its own reality show, complete with running commentary and occasional commercial breaks (usually when he zoned out in boring meetings).

Intrigued by this idea, RJ decided to lean into it. He began to consciously craft the narrative of his day, turning mundane tasks into epic quests:

"Our hero faces his greatest challenge yet - the Dishwasher of Doom! Armed only with his trusty sponge and an ancient bottle of dish soap, RJ must battle the forces of caked-on food and greasy residue.

Will he emerge victorious, or will he be forced to order takeout on paper plates for the rest of his days?"

His coworkers, unsurprisingly, found this new habit somewhat disconcerting:

"Uh, RJ?" his colleague Sarah asked one day. "Why are you narrating yourself walking down the hallway?"

RJ, caught in mid-narration ("...his footsteps echoing like the drums of an approaching army..."), blinked in surprise. "Oh, you know, just... staying mindful of my actions. Workplace mindfulness is very in right now, you know!"

Sarah raised an eyebrow. "Uh-huh. And does workplace mindfulness usually involve sound effects?"

RJ realized he might have gotten a bit carried away with his "whoosh" noises every time he turned a corner.

As he pondered this narrative approach to life, RJ couldn't help but wonder about its implications. If he was constantly telling his own story, did that mean he had some control over the plot? Could he rewrite the boring parts, or foreshadow exciting developments in upcoming chapters?

He experimented with this idea, trying to "write" a more exciting day for himself:

"Little did RJ know, as he entered the office that fateful Tuesday, that his life was about to change forever..."

He spent the rest of the day waiting for something dramatic to happen, eyeing his coworkers suspiciously and flinching every time someone opened the supply closet, half-expecting a plot twist to jump out at him.

By the end of the day, the only thing that had changed forever was the office coffee filter, but RJ remained undeterred. He was convinced that this narrative approach to life held some deeper truth.

"Maybe," he mused to Simon that evening, "the story we tell ourselves shapes our reality. Or maybe I've just had too much coffee and not enough human interaction. It's a philosophical toss-up, really."

As RJ continued to explore this idea of being the narrator of his own life, he found himself becoming more intentional about his choices and actions. After all, if he was the protagonist of his own story, shouldn't he strive to make it a tale worth telling?

This led to some interesting developments, like the time he decided his character arc needed more excitement:

"In a bold move to break out of his comfort zone, RJ decides to try a new lunch spot, venturing beyond the safe confines of his usual deli..."

Two hours and one questionable sandwich later:

"...and that, dear Simon," RJ groaned from his position on the couch, "is why the next chapter of our story will be set primarily in the bathroom. Let this be a lesson about the dangers of overly ambitious character development."

Despite the occasional misadventure, RJ found that thinking of his life as a narrative made him more aware of his personal growth, his relationships, and the way he faced challenges. He began to see himself not just as a programmer, but as a character on a journey, facing trials and tribulations, learning lessons, and (hopefully) approaching some form of enlightenment.

Or at least approaching a better understanding of when to narrate out loud and when to keep the story in his head. HR had some strong opinions about the appropriateness of sound effects during client meetings, it turned out.

As RJ drifted off to sleep that night, he couldn't help but smile. Life might be strange, confusing, and occasionally challenging, but at least it made for an interesting story. And as long as he was the one telling it, he might as well make it a tale worth hearing.

"And so," he mumbled sleepily, "our hero embarks on his next great adventure: a solid eight hours of sleep, uninterrupted by philosophical musings or ill-advised sandwich choices. Will he succeed? Tune in tomorrow to find out..."

With that, RJ fell asleep, his dreams a wild mix of narrative voiceovers, cosmic sandwiches, and a tap-dancing giraffe that bore a striking resemblance to Morgan Freeman. Just another chapter in the ongoing story of RJ, the self-talking philosopher-programmer extraordinaire. Imagine life as a never-ending story, authored by none other than ourselves. Through continuous self-talk, we construct this narrative, piece by piece. This ongoing internal narrative is an ever-present aspect of our consciousness. It's like having a personal narrator tagging along, whispering insights, judgments, and reflections in our mind.

The Morgan Effect

Let's think about how our inner narrator influences our perception and experience. Picture yourself walking through a park. Without your inner narrator, you'd merely see trees and hear birds. But with it, you might think, "What a lovely day! The sunshine feels warm on my skin." This narration colors your experience, adding layers of meaning to the simple act of walking. It's akin to watching a movie with and without commentary; the narrative brings depth and context to every scene - particularly if it is Mr Morgan 'himself' Freeman.

Self-talk serves as a lens through which we view the world. For instance, consider those moments when you face a challenge. If your inner narrator says, "I can handle this," you're likely to approach the situation with more confidence. On the flip side, if it whispers, "This is too hard," you may feel defeated before you've even begun. The voice in our heads shapes our reality, influencing not just how we see things but how we react to them as well.

Now, let's delve into the psychological aspects. There are both benefits and drawbacks to maintaining an internal story. One major benefit is enhanced self-awareness. When we narrate our lives, we're more attuned to our thoughts and feelings. This can lead to better understanding and management of emotions. For example, recognizing that you're feeling anxious because of a big presentation allows you to take steps to calm yourself.

However, there are potential downsides as well. Continuous self-talk can sometimes spiral into overthinking or negative thought patterns. Imagine constantly telling yourself, "I'm not good enough." This narrative can erode self-esteem and lead to anxiety or depression. It's like having a critical inner voice that never takes a break, constantly undermining your sense of worth.

People cope with life events using their internal narration in various ways. Take Jane, who recently lost her job. Her initial reaction might be panic: "I'll never find another job." But over time, she re-frames her narrative to something more empowering: "This is an opportunity to find something I love." This shift in self-talk helps her navigate the transition with a more positive outlook.

Similarly, athletes often use self-talk to enhance performance. Before a big game, a football player might mentally rehearse success: "I'll make that goal." This kind of positive self-narration boosts confidence and focus. It's like having a little cheerleader in your head, encouraging you to push harder and perform better.

In another scenario, people facing grief might find solace in their inner narrative. Suppose John has lost a loved one. His self-talk could initially be filled with sadness and regret: "I wish I had spent more time with them." Over time, however, he might start to remember the good times and say, "I'm grateful for all the memories we shared." This shift helps him move through his grief and find peace.

The idea of life as a narrative constructed through continuous selftalk is both fascinating and complex. It underscores the importance of being mindful of the stories we tell ourselves. After all, these narratives aren't just idle chit-chat in our minds; they shape our experiences, influence our mental health, and determine how we cope with challenges.

Our inner narrator is constantly at work, constructing the story of our lives. By becoming aware of this process, we gain the power to steer our narrative in positive directions. This doesn't mean ignoring negative emotions or pretending everything is perfect. Rather, it involves acknowledging our thoughts and feelings, then choosing to frame our narrative in a way that supports our well-being.

Think about it: next time you catch yourself in a loop of negative self-talk, try to re-frame the narrative. Instead of "I failed," consider saying, "I learned something valuable." This small shift can have a profound impact on your outlook and mental state.

It's also important to recognize that our internal narrator is influenced by various factors, including past experiences, beliefs, and even societal norms. By examining these influences, we can better understand why we tell certain stories and what changes we might need to make. This kind of introspection can lead to more authentic and empowering narratives.

Its a Wrap!

As RJ's self-talk increases, we've seen how it isn't just idle chatter but a powerful tool for introspection. From constantly analyzing his decisions to dissecting his emotions, RJ's internal dialogue plays a vital role in shaping his understanding of himself. This verbalization helps RJ clarify complex thoughts and gain new perspectives, making it easier to identify patterns and root causes behind his feelings. Whether it's pondering personal experiences or preparing for challenging tasks, RJ's self-talk offers valuable cognitive insights that enhance his decision-making and emotional regulation.

Moreover, this process of turning spontaneous self-talk into structured reflection signifies a deeper level of introspection. RJ isn't merely talking to himself for company; he's using these conversations as a mental playground for exploring life's bigger questions. By adapting his internal dialogue to different contexts and consciously shifting from negative to positive language, RJ can navigate life's complexities more effectively. So, the next time you catch yourself having a conversation with your inner narrator, remember you're not just muttering to yourself—you're engaging in a transformative journey towards greater self-awareness and personal growth.

Part VII: Future Talk and Spreading the Word

The Future of Self-Talk: RJ's Tech-Savvy Speculations

RJ's self-talk is a fascinating blend of internal dialogue, introspection, and occasional bursts of humor. Picture RJ navigating his day with an ongoing commentary that ranges from motivational pep talks to deep dives into the meaning of life. Part VII unravels the many layers of technology and futuristic magnificence.

As RJ's self-talk journey continued, his programmer's mind couldn't help but wander into the realm of future possibilities. What would self-talk look like in a world of advancing technology? Would AI assistants join the conversation? Could virtual reality transform internal dialogue into a full-sensory experience? RJ was determined to find out – or at least, to come up with some wildly entertaining theories.

Crystal Ballin: RJ's TechSpeculations

As RJ's self-talk journey continued, his programmer's mind couldn't help but wander into the realm of future possibilities. What would self-talk look like in a world of advancing technology? Would AI assistants join the conversation? Could virtual reality transform internal dialogue into a full-sensory experience? RJ was determined to find out – or at least, to come up with some wildly entertaining theories.

AI Assistants: The New Voices in Our Heads

One morning, as RJ was having his usual chat with his coffee maker (which, to be fair, was more of a one-sided plea for caffeine), a thought struck him:

"What if, in the future, AI assistants become advanced enough to engage in our self-talk?"

The idea was both exciting and mildly terrifying, like discovering you can fly but only over shark-infested waters.

RJ imagined a future where everyone had a personalized AI assistant living in their brain, ready to chime in with facts, advice, and possibly unsolicited movie recommendations:

RJ: "I wonder if I should ask Sarah out on a date?"

AI Assistant: "Based on your previous interactions, there's a 68% chance she'll say yes. However, I must warn you that your joke repertoire is severely outdated. Shall I download the latest dad jokes for you?"

RJ: "No, no, that won't be nece—"

AI Assistant: "Download complete. Would you like to hear a joke about paper? It's tearable."

RJ: "I immediately regret this feature."

As RJ pondered this potential future, he couldn't help but wonder about the implications. Would we become overly dependent on our AI thought-partners? Would we forget how to make decisions without consulting our digital brain-buddies?

"Then again," RJ mused, "it might be nice to have someone to blame for my bad decisions. Sorry I'm late for work – my AI assistant miscalculated the traffic patterns while daydreaming about electric sheep."

Virtual Reality Self-Talk: A Meta Mind Palace for the Masses

As RJ's futuristic speculations continued, he stumbled upon another intriguing possibility: self-talk in virtual reality. What about the Cryptoverse?

"Imagine," he said excitedly to Simon the cockatiel, who was looking increasingly concerned about his owner's sanity, "a virtual environment where you could visualize your thoughts, interact with different aspects of your personality, and literally build thought castles in the air whilst owning all your assets as NFT's!"

RJ envisioned a world where people could put on a VR headset and step into a personalized mindscape. Need to make a tough decision?

Why not convene a virtual board meeting with all your inner voices? He imagined his own VR mind-space:

The scene: A futuristic boardroom. Seated around the table are holograms representing different aspects of RJ's personality. Logic Lad is wearing a Spock costume, Worry Wally is wrapped in a security blanket, Creative Carl is painting on the walls, and Motivated Mary is jogging in place.

RJ: "Okay, team, we need to decide whether to take on this new project at work."

Logic Lad: "The pros and cons are clear. I've prepared a 700-slide PowerPoint presentation to—"

Creative Carl: "Boring! Let's interpretive dance our decision!"

Worry Wally: "But what if we dance badly and everyone laughs at us and we're fired and end up living in a cardboard box?"

Motivated Mary: "We can live in the best darn cardboard box this side of the Mississippi! Let's do this!"

RJ chuckled at the thought. "It would certainly make self-talk more entertaining," he mused. "Although, knowing me, I'd probably spend more time designing my virtual mind-office than actually making decisions."

Thought-to-Text Technology: When Inner Voices Become Bestsellers

As RJ continued to ponder the future of self-talk, another idea struck him – what if technology could transcribe our inner dialogues directly into text?

"Think about it, Simon," RJ said excitedly to his feathered confidant. "We could turn our stream of consciousness into books, blogs, or extremely confusing Twitter feeds!"

He imagined a world where people could publish their unfiltered thoughts in real-time:

Best-Selling Books of 2050:

1.   "**To Lunch or Not to Lunch** : A Software Developer's Internal Food Debate" by RJ Smith

2.   " **The Girl with the Quantum Brain: A Physicist's Inner Monologue** " by RJ Wilson

3.   " **Fifty Shades of Beige: An Interior Designer's Stressful Journey Through Color Swatches** " by RJ Bored

"Of course," RJ mused, "this technology could lead to some awkward situations. Imagine your inner critique of your boss's presentation being broadcasted to the entire office. We'd have to develop some serious mental privacy settings."

As RJ's mind buzzed with these futuristic possibilities, he couldn't help but feel a mix of excitement and trepidation. The future of selftalk seemed bright, if a bit overwhelming. But then again, wasn't that true of all progress?

"Well, Simon," RJ said, leaning back in his chair, "the future of selftalk might be high-tech, but I have a feeling we'll always need the good old-fashioned art of talking to ourselves. After all, someone needs to tell our AI assistants when their jokes are bad."

Teaching Others: RJ's Mission to Spread the Gospel of Self-Talk

Empowered by his self-talk journey and armed with futuristic speculations, RJ decided it was time to share his wisdom with the world. Or at least with his somewhat reluctant friends and colleagues. It was time for RJ to become a self-talk evangelist! What about X?

The Lunch Break Lectures: RJ's Coworkers Become Unwitting Students

RJ's first attempts at spreading the word about self-talk happened organically – or as his coworkers might say, unavoidably – during lunch breaks.

"Did you know," RJ would say, mouth full of sandwich, "that talking to yourself can improve your problem-solving skills by up to 30%?"

His colleague, Jim, looked up from his salad, a mix of confusion and concern on his face. "Uh, is that a real statistic?"

"Well, I just made it up," RJ admitted, "but it feels true, doesn't it? That's the power of positive self-talk!"

Despite the initial skepticism, RJ's enthusiasm was infectious. Soon, he had a small but curious audience for his lunchtime lectures on the benefits of self-talk.

"Today's topic," RJ announced one afternoon, standing up and straightening an imaginary tie, "is using different voices for different aspects of your personality. I call it 'The Inner Avengers Initiative'."

As RJ launched into an explanation of how to assemble a mental team of inner voices, complete with superhero analogies, his coworkers exchanged glances that ranged from amused to mildly worried.

"And remember," RJ concluded, "your inner Hulk should only come out when you're debugging particularly nasty code!"

The Self-Talk Support Group: RJ's Attempt at Community Building

Encouraged by the (mostly polite) reception to his lunchtime lectures, RJ decided to take things a step further. He posted flyers around the office: "Join the Self-Talk Support Group! Because talking to yourself is better with company!"

The first meeting was... sparsely attended. In fact, the only attendee was Carl from Accounting, who admitted he had misread the flyer and thought it was a group for self-taught folk dancing.

Undeterred, RJ decided to proceed with the meeting anyway.

"Welcome, Carl! Today, we'll be exploring the art of positive selfaffirmations. Repeat after me: I am a spreadsheet wizard!"

Carl, looking increasingly confused but too polite to leave, mumbled along.

By the end of the hour, Carl might not have become a self-talk convert, but he had learned three new Excel shortcuts and gained a newfound appreciation for the power of a well-timed internal pep talk.

"Same time next week?" RJ asked hopefully.

"I'll, uh, check my schedule," Carl replied, backing slowly towards the door.

The Viral Video Venture: RJ's Foray into Online Education

Realizing that his in-person efforts might be limiting his reach, RJ decided to take his teachings to the internet. He set up a camera in his living room and prepared to film his first self-talk tutorial video. "Welcome to 'Talk the Talk with RJ'!" he began, flashing a thumbsup at the camera. "Today, we'll be learning how to debug your negative self-talk! Remember, if your inner voice is being a jerk, it's time for a code review!"

RJ proceeded to demonstrate various self-talk techniques, using different voices and occasionally rope in a very reluctant Simon the cockatiel as a prop.

"And that's how you turn 'I can't do this' into 'I'm learning to do this'! Tune in next time when we'll explore 'Rubber Duck Debugging: Not Just for Code Anymore'!"

To RJ's surprise (and mild terror), the video went viral. Suddenly, he was fielding calls from morning shows and fielding questions from an army of new followers:

"How do I optimize my inner voice's bandwidth?"

"Can I outsource my negative self-talk to a call center?"

"Is it cultural appropriation if my inner voice speaks with a British accent?"

As RJ navigated his newfound internet fame, he couldn't help but feel a sense of accomplishment. Sure, some people thought he was eccentric, and he was pretty sure his mom was responsible for at least half of his video views, but he was spreading the word about self-talk!

"You know, Simon," RJ said one evening, scrolling through comments on his latest video, "I think we're really making a difference. We're changing the world, one internal monologue at a time!"

Simon, as usual, simply squawked and demanded a cracker.

As RJ's mission to teach others about self-talk continued, he faced challenges, skepticism, and the occasional viral meme featuring his most embarrassing on-camera moments. But through it all, he

remained convinced of one thing: the world would be a better place if
everyone learned to have a good chat with themselves now and then.

"After all," RJ mused as he prepared for his next video, "in a world full
of noise, sometimes the most important voice to listen to is your own.
Especially if that voice is telling you it's time to take a break and have
a snack. Inner wisdom comes in many forms!"

And with that profound (if slightly hunger-influenced) thought, RJ
turned to the camera, flashed his signature thumbs-up, and prepared
to enlighten the internet once more about the wonders of self-talk. The
future of internal dialogue was bright, and RJ was determined to be its
somewhat awkward, always enthusiastic guide.

Penultimate Reflections

In this final part of RJ's self-talk odyssey, our intrepid programmer
turns his attention to the future and takes on the role of an enthusiastic
(if somewhat awkward) self-talk evangelist.

The Future of Self-Talk: RJ's Tech-Savvy Speculations

RJ's vivid imagination and tech background collide as he envisions the
future of self-talk in a world of advancing technology:

AI Assistants: RJ imagines a future where personalized AI assistants
join our internal dialogues, offering advice, facts, and possibly
unsolicited dad jokes. He ponders the benefits and potential pitfalls of
having a digital thought-partner, including the luxury of blaming bad
decisions on your AI.

Virtual Reality Self-Talk: Taking self-talk to a whole new dimension, RJ envisions VR environments where people can visualize their thoughts and interact with different aspects of their personality.

Picture a virtual board meeting with your inner voices, where Logic Lad presents PowerPoint slides and Creative Carl suggests interpretive dance as a decision-making tool.

Thought-to-Text Technology: RJ speculates about technology that could transcribe our inner dialogues directly into text, leading to a world of stream-of-consciousness books and potentially awkward social situations. He imagines bestseller lists filled with titles like "To Lunch or Not to Lunch: A Software Developer's Internal Food Debate."

Teaching Others: RJ's Mission to Spread the Gospel of Self-Talk

Excited by his self-talk journey, RJ takes it upon himself to share his wisdom with the world:

The Lunch Break Lectures: RJ's first attempts at teaching happen during office lunch breaks, where he regales his bemused colleagues with self-talk tips and dubious statistics. His enthusiasm is infectious, even if his "Inner Avengers Initiative" leaves some coworkers questioning their lunch venue choices.

The Self-Talk Support Group: Undeterred by low attendance (read: one confused accountant who thought it was a folk dancing class), RJ forges ahead with his support group. While he might not have created a self-talk revolution, he did improve Carl from Accounting's Excel skills and appreciation for internal pep talks.

The Viral Video Venture: RJ takes his teachings online, creating selftalk tutorial videos that unexpectedly go viral. Suddenly, he's fielding questions from an army of new followers, including inquiries about optimizing inner voice bandwidth and the cultural implications of internal British accents.

Throughout his efforts to teach others, RJ faces skepticism, challenges, and the occasional viral meme featuring his most embarrassing on-camera moments. But he remains convinced that the world would be a better place if everyone learned to have a good chat with themselves now and then.

As RJ navigates his newfound internet fame and continues his mission to spread the word about self-talk, he reflects on the journey that brought him here. From a frustrated programmer talking to his code to a self-talk guru with a viral online presence, RJ's adventure proves that sometimes, the most important voice to listen to is your own — especially when it's telling you it's time for a snack break.

In the end, RJ's exploration of future self-talk technologies and his earnest (if sometimes misguided) attempts to teach others serve as a fitting conclusion to his journey. It reminds us that whether we're talking to ourselves with the help of futuristic tech or simply muttering under our breath, the power of self-talk lies not in how we do it, but in the insights, comfort, and occasional laughs it brings us along the way.

Conclusion

Final Thoughts: Embracing the Conversation Within

As RJ sat in his favorite coffee shop, sipping a latte and engaging in what onlookers might mistake for an animated conversation with an invisible friend, he couldn't help but marvel at the journey that had brought him here. From accidental mutterings to full-blown internal debates, from social awkwardness to viral video stardom, RJ's adventure in self-talk had been nothing short of extraordinary.

"Well, old chap," RJ said to himself, ignoring the curious glances from nearby patrons, "we've certainly come a long way, haven't we?"

Indeed, they had. RJ reflected on the key lessons he'd learned along his chatty path:

1. **The Power of Inner Dialogue**: What had started as a quirky habit had become a valuable tool for problem-solving, creativity, and emotional regulation. RJ now approached challenges with a mental team of experts – Logic Lad, Creative Carl, and Motivated Mary were always ready to chime in with their unique perspectives.

1. **The Importance of Positive Self-Talk**: RJ had learned to be his own cheerleader, turning his inner critic into a constructive feedback partner. "We've gone from 'You're an idiot' to 'You're learning and growing,'" RJ mused. "Though we still occasionally add 'you beautiful idiot' for old times' sake."

1. **The Balance of Internal and External Communication**: While RJ had embraced his self-talk, he'd also learned the importance of external dialogue. His attempts to teach others had shown him the value of sharing ideas and connecting with people – even if it sometimes resulted in viral videos of his most embarrassing moments.

1. **The Future is Bright (Possibly Very Chatty)**: RJ's speculations about the future of self-talk had opened up exciting possibilities. While he was still waiting for his AI inner voice assistant (he was hoping for one with Morgan Freeman's voice), he was excited about the potential for technology to enhance our internal dialogues.

1. **The Universality of Self-Talk**: Through his journey, RJ had discovered that talking to oneself wasn't just a personal quirk – it was a fundamental human experience. Whether through internal whispers or full-blown conversations with coffee mugs, people everywhere were engaging in self-talk.

As RJ pondered these insights, he realized that his journey had transformed not just how he talked to himself, but how he approached life. He was more self-aware, more resilient, and, if he was being honest, probably more entertaining at parties (even if he was mostly entertaining himself).

"You know," RJ said, leaning back in his chair, "maybe the real treasure was the friends we made along the way – and by friends, I mean the various aspects of our personality that we've gotten to know."

Just then, a small child at a nearby table pointed at RJ and loudly asked, "Mommy, why is that man talking to himself?"

RJ, without missing a beat, turned to the child with a wink and said, "I'm having a meeting with my board of directors. They all live up here," he tapped his temple, "and let me tell you, they can be a handful - its new technology that helps me!"

The child's eyes widened with wonder, and RJ could swear he saw a flicker of recognition in the mother's eyes. Maybe, just maybe, he had inspired another person to embrace their inner dialogue.

As RJ left the coffee shop, he felt a sense of contentment wash over him. His journey through the world of self-talk had been filled with laughter, learning, and the occasional public embarrassment, but he wouldn't have had it any other way.

"Well, RJ," he said as he walked down the street, "what's next on our agenda?"

"World domination?" his inner Creative Carl suggested.

"Perhaps something a bit more realistic," countered Logic Lad.

"How about we start with making dinner without burning the kitchen down?" Worry Wally chimed in.

"Buy some more Bitcoin?" said future RJ.

RJ chuckled. "One step at a time, team. One step at a time."

"Hey what, ...Bitcoin, where did you come from future RJ?."

"Not where but 'when' did I arrive my friend!."

And so, our self-talking hero continued on his way, ready to face whatever challenges life might throw at him. After all, with a head full of chatty companions and a heart full of self-acceptance, RJ knew he was ready for anything.

As he disappeared around the corner, still deep in conversation with himself, one thing was clear: RJ might talk to himself too much, but in doing so, he had found his voice, his strength, and his own unique way of navigating the world.

And really, isn't that what life's all about? Finding your voice – even if it's the one inside your head.

"Especially if it's the one inside your head," RJ corrected himself with a grin. "Now, about that dinner..."

"How many should we invite Simon?."

"Cracker!"

THE END

In conclusion, the journey we've shared with RJ has been both enlightening and entertaining. We've delved deep into the significant role self-talk plays in our daily lives, unraveling the mysteries and benefits of this often-overlooked conversation within. RJ's ability to weave humor through serious introspection has not only made these concepts more accessible but also much more enjoyable.

Finding balance in life can feel like juggling flaming swords while riding a unicycle across a tightrope. RJ's experience in integrating healthy self-talk into their daily routine shows that it's not only possible but also incredibly beneficial. By turning up the volume on positive affirmations and dialing down the weight of negative chatter, RJ has crafted a balanced mindset capable of tackling life's ups and downs with grace—and a dash of wit. The key takeaway is the realization that self-talk is an ongoing dialogue, not a monologue. It's about engaging with oneself as you would with a good friend: supportive, honest, and occasionally hilarious.

This brings us to a universal truth RJ stumbled upon—self-talk is a shared human trait. Everybody does it. Whether it's prepping for a big presentation, debating that extra slice of pizza, or just mulling over life's existential questions, we're all conversing internally. Recognizing this shared experience helps us feel less isolated in our inner dialogues. RJ's humorous take on these moments reminds us that we can find camaraderie in our quirks and that sometimes, laughing at ourselves is the best therapy.

Looking ahead, the potential applications and research in the field of self-talk are as vast as they are exciting. Imagine a world where we harness the power of positive self-talk to boost mental health, enhance productivity, and foster resilient mindsets from an early age. Schools could integrate self-talk strategies into their curriculum, teaching kids to approach challenges with a growth mindset. Workplaces might offer workshops on effective selfdialogue to improve employee well-being and performance. Further research could even uncover new techniques for optimizing self-talk, tailored to individual needs and lifestyles. The possibilities are endless, and RJ's story serves as an inspiring starting point for what could be a broader societal shift towards valuing and cultivating healthier inner conversations.

Reflecting on RJ's journey, we see a roadmap of personal growth filled with insights and revelations. At the outset, RJ's self-talk was like an old mixtape stuck on repeat—playing the same tired tunes of doubt, fear, and negativity. But through experimentation, perseverance, and no small amount of humor, RJ managed to remix those tracks into an empowering playlist that celebrates strengths, acknowledges weaknesses, and fuels motivation. This transformation wasn't overnight—it was a series of small, deliberate steps, each one building on the last. It's a testament to the idea that profound change comes not from grand gestures but from consistent, mindful practices.

RJ's story is a reminder that our inner dialogue wields immense power over our perception and reality. By becoming aware of our self-talk patterns and consciously guiding them towards positivity, we can drastically alter our emotional and psychological landscape. It emphasizes the importance of being kind to ourselves, of cutting ourselves some slack, and of using humor as a tool to navigate the complexities of life.

As we close this chapter, let's carry forward the lessons learned from RJ's experience. Embrace your inner conversation, listen intently, and steer it towards positivity. Find balance by acknowledging both the good and the bad while choosing to focus on growth. Remember, self-talk is a shared human trait—you're never alone in your internal musings. And finally, keep an eye on future developments in selftalk research; there's always more to learn and ways to improve.

So go ahead, strike up a conversation with yourself. Make it meaningful, make it positive, and most importantly, make it fun.

After all, who better to chat with than the person who knows you best? And if you ever need inspiration, just think back to RJ's journey – a testament to the transformative power of embracing the conversation within, one laughter at a time.